The Bee Who Did A Wee

and Other Funny Stories

By Phil Jay

Copyright © 2023 Phil Jay
All Rights Reserved.

THE DUCK WHO HAD NO LUCK

In a peaceful pond nestled in the heart of Sunnyvale, there lived a duck named Disco. Now, Disco was not your ordinary duck. He had an unusual talent for attracting the silliest and most hilarious situations, earning him the nickname "Disco the Unlucky Duck." No matter where he waddled, mischief and laughter followed.

One morning, Disco set out on a quest to find the tastiest breadcrumbs in the whole pond. As he quacked his way through the reeds, his feathers glimmering in the sunlight, he couldn't help but feel a little mischievous. Little did he know that the mischievousness was about to catch up with him. As Disco reached the edge of the pond, he spotted a group of children having a picnic. Their basket was overflowing with delicious treats, and Disco's beak watered with anticipation. Sneaking up, he slyly tried to swipe a crumb from the basket, but just as he was about to snatch it, he slipped on a banana peel lying on the ground!

Quacking loudly, Disco tumbled head over tail and landed in the middle of the picnic blanket, causing quite a fuss. The children burst into laughter, rolling on the grass and pointing at Disco, who now had a sandwich stuck on his beak. Embarrassed but determined to make the best of the situation, Disco decided to join in the fun. He started dancing around with the sandwich on his beak, performing silly twirls and spins. The children giggled and clapped, cheering him on as if he were the star of a big performance.

Just as Disco was taking in all the applause, a gust of wind swooped in, snatching the sandwich off his beak and sending it soaring into the air! Disco the Duck watched helplessly as the sandwich flew higher and higher until it disappeared into the clouds. The children erupted into fits of laughter, unable to contain their amusement.

Feeling a little sad, Disco waddled back to the pond, his feathers drooping with disappointment. But as he reached the water's edge, a group of cute young ducklings swam up to him, their eyes sparkling with admiration. They had witnessed his hilarious escapade and wanted to learn his silly dance moves.

Disco began teaching the ducklings his signature twirls and spins. Soon, the pond echoed with quacks and the sound of little webbed feet stomping in rhythm. Disco had unintentionally become the greatest dance instructor in the animal kingdom, spreading laughter and happiness wherever he went. Disco the unlucky duck learned that luck wasn't about avoiding mishaps, but about embracing them with a smile. From that day on, he continued to waddle through life, making everyone laugh and reminding them that even in the funniest of failures, there was always a silver lining. Disco really did love to make everyone laugh out loud!

THE RABBIT WHO HAD A BAD HABIT

In a cozy rabbit burrow tucked away under the ground, there lived a rabbit named Robbie. Robbie the rabbit was a mischievous and playful rabbit, but he had a funny habit that often got him into trouble. This is the tale of Robbie, the rabbit with a bad habit.

Robbie's bad habit was none other than his love for carrots. While most rabbits enjoyed a carrot here and there, Robbie simply couldn't get enough. He nibbled on carrots day and night, munching through piles of them with a voracious appetite. He just loved to eat carrots all the time!

Now, you might think that there's nothing wrong with a rabbit loving carrots. But Robbie's obsession had a comical twist. Whenever he ate too many carrots, Robbie turned an astonishing shade of bright orange! His fur, his whiskers, even his fluffy tail transformed into a vibrant hue that stood out like a carrot in a haystack. He was like a big rabbit shaped lamp running around the place!

The other woodland creatures couldn't help but chuckle at Robbie's unusual appearance. Squirrels chattered, birds tweeted, and even the wise old owl hooted with laughter whenever Robbie hopped by. But Robbie didn't mind one bit. In fact, he embraced his unique colour and saw it as an opportunity to excitement to the forest.

On day Robbie decided to have a little fun with his bad habit. He sneaked into Farmer McGregor's carrot patch, where the most delicious and plump carrots grew. Robbie's eyes widened with excitement as he hopped from row to row, gorging on carrots like there was no tomorrow. He kept a close eye out for Mr McGregor to ensure he wouldn't be seen. Look around you right now, keep quiet and sneak closely, must not let me be seen Robbie thought to himself.

Farmer McGregor had set up a scarecrow to guard his precious carrots. As Robbie munched away, the scarecrow suddenly sprang to life, flapping its arms and scaring the wits out of poor Robbie. He jumped so high in surprise that he landed right in the middle of the carrot patch, buried up to his fluffy tail in freshly tilled soil! This sight was too much for the woodland creatures to handle. They rolled on the ground, tears streaming down their faces, unable to contain their laughter. Even the usually composed squirrel couldn't resist snorting with mirth.

Robbie, covered in soil and carrots, joined in the laughter too. He hopped out of the patch, leaving a trail of orange pawprints behind him. Embracing his newfound disguise as a carrot-covered rabbit, Robbie bounced through the forest, pretending to be a "Carrot Monster" and giving his friends a good chase. Robbie thought to himself, 'well, its Farmer McGregor who is going to be afraid of me now, ha!'

The animals ran in all directions, trying to avoid being caught by the mischievous Carrot Monster. Robbie hopped, skipped, and giggled, leading the animals on a wild chase through the forest, with orange fluff flying in every direction. Eventually, the animals caught up to Robbie and surrounded him. He had succeeded in bringing smiles to everyone's faces, and his bad habit had turned into a source of endless laughter. Robbie's carrot obsession continued, and he remained the carrot-covered joker of the forest. Whenever someone needed a good laugh, they knew just where to find Robbie and his mischievous adventures. Plus, if the electric went off and anyone needed a light, everyone knew to fill Robbie the rabbit with some carrots!

THE PONY WHO WAS ALWAYS MOANY

Percy the pony was known far and wide for his moaning and groaning. He had a knack for finding something to complain about, no matter the situation. From the moment Percy woke up in his cozy stable, he would let out a loud, dramatic sigh. "Oh, what a terrible night's sleep! My hay was too prickly, my blanket was too itchy, and the moonlight was too bright. I'm positively exhausted!" he'd moan, much to the amusement of the other animals.

As Percy trotted through the meadow, he would spot a patch of flowers. Instead of admiring their beauty like the other ponies, Percy would grumble, "Why are these flowers so colourful? They hurt my eyes! And they have such a strong scent. It's positively suffocating!"

Even the weather couldn't escape Percy's complaints. On sunny days, he'd whine, "It's far too hot! I'm sweating like a pig, or should I say, like a pony!" And when it rained, he'd moan, "The rain is ruining my perfect mane! I'll never be able to show my face in public!"

One day, the other animals in the meadow decided they had enough of Percy's constant moaning. They gathered together for an emergency meeting to come up with a plan to cheer him up and make him see the humour in life. First, the mischievous squirrels orchestrated a hilarious acorn chase, leading Percy on a wild goose (or rather, squirrel) chase. They darted through the trees, chattering and giggling, while Percy huffed and puffed, trying to catch them. Eventually, he found himself tangled in a bush, and the squirrels couldn't contain their laughter.

Next, the birds organized a feather fashion show, where they adorned themselves with colourful feathers and paraded around in front of Percy. They strutted their stuff, twirling and chirping, while Percy watched, unable to resist a smile. The sight of the birds flaunting their feathery finery was too silly to ignore.

But the grand finale of the plan involved the wise old owl, who was known for his wisdom and wit. The owl invited Percy for a late-night chat under the moonlight. As they sat on a branch, the owl began telling the most uproarious jokes and puns, one after another. He had Percy laughing so hard that tears streamed down his face.

From that night on, Percy began to see the funny side of things. He even started sharing his own jokes, albeit with a touch of moaning mixed in. The animals would gather around, waiting for Percy's latest groaning punchline. As Percy's moans turned into laughter, the meadow became a livelier place. The animals joined in the fun, telling jokes, playing pranks, and finding laughter in the smallest of moments. And whenever Percy felt a complaint bubbling up inside him, he would pause, take a deep breath, and join in the laughter instead.

THE KANGAROO WHO HAD NO CLUE

In the vast and wild plains of Australia, there lived a kangaroo named Joey. Joey was a cheerful and lovable kangaroo, but he had one funny issue, he was as clueless as can be. While his kangaroo friends hopped and bounded across the land with agility and purpose, Joey was often found staring blankly into space, his mind lost in a world of its own.

Joey's cluelessness had been a lifelong challenge. Even as a little joey, he would hop in the wrong direction, often ending up in the most absurd situations. His friends would chuckle and shake their heads as Joey attempted to grasp even the simplest concepts of kangaroo life. One sunny day, as the kangaroos gathered near a watering hole, Joey decided it was time to embark on an adventure. He bounded up to his friends and announced, "I have a brilliant idea! Let's explore the Great Outback!"

The kangaroos exchanged looks at each other. While they were used to Joey's funny ways, they couldn't help but wonder what kind of chaos he would unleash this time. Joey hopped off into the Outback, with his friends following close behind, curious to see what misadventures lay ahead. They bounced around the red sand and tall green forests, meeting many creatures along the way.

Joey's first encounter was with a wise old emu. "Hello, Joey! What brings you to the Outback today?" the emu asked. "I'm on a quest to find the legendary Fountain of Hops!" Joey declared, his eyes shining with excitement. The emu chuckled, realizing that Joey had mixed up his words yet again. "Joey, it's called the Fountain of Youth, not the Fountain of Hops! But I admire your excitement."

Joey nodded and thanked the emu, completely unaware of his blunder. He continued on, hopping through the Outback, leaving his bemused friends in stitches behind him. As they continued their journey, they stumbled upon a group of koalas perched lazily on a tree. Joey looked up at them and said, "G'day, mates! I'm searching for the mystical Tree of Snacks. Have any of you seen it?"

The koalas exchanged bewildered glances. "Joey, it's called the Tree of Life, not the Tree of Snacks," one of them replied, barely able to contain their laughter. Joey scratched his head in confusion, oblivious to his mistake. "Ah, yes! The Tree of Life. That's what I meant! Thanks, mates!"

As Joey and his friends ventured deeper into the Outback, they stumbled upon a shimmering pool of water and right there stood a beautiful kangaroo named Matilda, with sleek fur and twinkling eyes.

Joey's heart skipped a beat as he laid eyes on Matilda. He hopped over, trying to impress her with his adventurous tales. "Matilda, my dear, I have journeyed far and wide in search of the legendary... uh... well, let's just say I've been on an incredible quest!" Matilda smiled, charmed by Joey's enthusiasm. "Oh, really? And what have you discovered on your incredible quest?"

Joey puffed out his chest and proudly proclaimed, "I have found the legendary... um... the... you know, the... oh, never mind! I haven't found anything, but I'm having a jolly good time!"

Matilda giggled and placed a paw on Joey's shoulder. "Joey, it's not about finding something extraordinary. It's about embracing the joy of the journey itself."
Joey's face lit up with understanding, finally grasping the essence of Matilda's words. "You're right, Matilda! It's not about the destination, but the adventure along the way!"

Joey and his friends continued to explore the Outback, hopping and bounding with reckless abandon.

Joey may have been clueless, but his endearing nature and infectious enthusiasm brought joy and laughter to all who crossed his path. And as he hopped into the sunset, his friends realized that sometimes, it's the clueless ones who teach us the most and that laughter is the best companion on any adventure.

THE SLOTH WHO HAD A COUGH

Stanley was known for his slow and leisurely nature, spending his days hanging from tree branches, seemingly motionless. But one day, a strange thing happened to Stanley that turned his world upside down — he developed a cough!

It all began with a little tickle in Stanley's throat. At first, he ignored it, thinking it was just a temporary irritation. But as the days went by, the tickle grew into a full-blown cough. And not just any cough, mind you. It was a cough that echoed through the rainforest, causing the birds to pause mid-flight and the monkeys to drop their bananas in surprise.

Word of Stanley's cough spread through the rainforest like wildfire. The other animals gathered around, their eyes wide with curiosity. Sloths were known for their slow and silent existence, so a coughing sloth was an extraordinary sight. The mischievous monkeys, always up for a laugh, swung from branch to branch, imitating Stanley's cough with exaggerated theatrics. They scratched their throats, contorted their faces, and let out a series of exaggerated coughs, causing the rainforest to erupt in laughter.

Stanley, who was not used to being the center of attention, blushed with embarrassment. He tried to hide behind his long fur, hoping that the cough would soon disappear and he could return to his peaceful slowness he was used to. But the cough had other plans. It kept on going, much to Stanley's dismay. He tried everything to soothe it — from drinking herbal remedies made by the wise old owl to wrapping his throat in moss, but nothing seemed to work. The cough became louder and more boisterous, as if it had a life of its own.

The other animals, intrigued by Stanley's situation, started offering their own "cough remedies." The chattering parrots recommended singing at the top of his lungs, while the wise old owl suggested meditating under the moonlight. Even the squirrels claimed that a diet of acorns would miraculously cure the cough.

Stanley, desperate for relief, decided to try every remedy thrown his way. So, there he was, hanging from a branch, singing songs at the top of his lungs while munching on acorns, all in a desperate attempt to silence his cough.

The rainforest had never seen such a spectacle. The animals gathered around, unable to contain their laughter. Monkeys swung from the trees, imitating Stanley's singing and coughing. Birds chirped and squawked, their feathers ruffling from the vibrations of laughter.

But just when Stanley thought things couldn't get any worse, a group of toucans, with their colourful beaks and mischievous grins, decided to join the fun. They formed a "cough choir," each toucan imitating Stanley's cough in perfect harmony. The rainforest erupted in uproarious laughter, the sound echoing through the trees.

Stanley, now thoroughly tired and fed up, let out a loud, really loud cough, almost as if he was joining in on the joke. And to his surprise, the animals around him fell silent. They looked at Stanley, then at each other, and burst into a fit of laughter that shook the very branches of the rainforest.

In that moment, Stanley realized he had unwittingly become the comedian of the rainforest, with his cough as the punchline.

Embracing his newfound role, Stanley continued to cough, letting out exaggerated coughs that left the animals in stitches. He even learned to add a little dance to his cough, swaying from side to side with each silly burst. The rainforest animals couldn't get enough of Stanley's comedic performances, and they would gather around him, waiting for the next round of laughter.

THE GIRAFFE WITH THE FUNNY LAUGH

Gerald was not your ordinary giraffe. Besides his long neck and graceful stride, he had a laugh that was simply out of this world. It was a laugh that could startle zebras from their stripes and make lions forget their roars. Yes, Gerald had a funny laugh, and it was about to lead him on an adventure filled with uproarious laughter and unexpected twists.

One morning, Gerald was stretching his long legs and munching on the juiciest leaves, he heard a faint giggle coming from behind a cluster of trees. He slowly moved his neck and peeked around the corner of a tree, only to discover a family of mischievous monkeys, their tails twitching with mischief.

Gerald approached the monkeys and asked, "Hey there, what's so funny?"

The monkeys looked up at him, their eyes gleaming with mischief. "Oh, Gerald, you have no idea how funny you are," said Momo, the cheekiest of the bunch. "Your laugh, my friend, is legendary. It's the stuff of savannah tales and jungle stories."

Gerald blinked his large, expressive eyes, a hint of confusion on his face. "My laugh? What's so special about it?"

The monkeys exchanged knowing glances and burst into laughter. They rolled on the ground, their tails flailing in the air, barely able to catch their breath. Gerald couldn't help but feel a little self-conscious, wondering what was so hilarious about his laugh.

Finally, when the monkeys had calmed down, Momo wiped away a tear of laughter and said, "Gerald, my friend, your laugh is so silly. It starts as a gentle giggle, builds up to a snort, and ends with a burst. We monkeys can't resist it! We want to share it with the whole savannah!"

Gerald's worry about the monkeys melted away, replaced by a sense of pride. He realized that his funny laugh could bring joy to the animals. With a twinkle in his eye and a bounce in his step, Gerald decided to embark on a mission to spread laughter throughout the land. The news of Gerald's hilarious laugh spread like wildfire across the savannah. Animals from far and wide gathered in anticipation of the laughter that awaited them. Zebras lined up in neat rows, lions adjusted their manes, and even the elephants perked up their enormous ears, eager to witness the spectacle.

As the animals at a watering hole waited, Gerald stood tall and let out his first laugh. It started as a gentle chuckle, causing a ripple of smiles among the zebras. But as it grew, the chuckle turned into a snort, and before long, the savannah was filled with the crazy roars of laughter.

The hyenas rolled on the ground, their sides splitting from laughter. The elephants trumpeted with glee, their enormous bodies shaking the ground. Even the rhinos couldn't help but crack a smile, their tough exterior crumbling in the face of Gerald's infectious laugh.

But the laughter didn't stop there. The sound carried beyond the wild of the natural park, reaching the depths of the jungle and the peaks of the mountains. Monkeys swung from the treetops, squirrels chattered with delight, and birds chirped a merry tune.

As the laughter subsided, Gerald looked around at the animals, tears of joy streaming down their faces. The savannah had transformed into a paradise of laughter, where worries and troubles were forgotten, and the only thing that mattered was the sound of pure joy. From that day on, Gerald became known as the Giraffe with the Funny Laugh. Animals from far and wide would travel to the savannah just to witness his infectious chuckles and snorts. They would gather around, sharing stories, jokes, and laughter until the sun dipped below the horizon.

THE SNAKE WHO ATE THE CAKE

Sammy was not your average snake. While other snakes slithered around, hunting for mice and basking in the sun, Sammy had a unique appetite — he had a massive craving for cake! Yes, you heard that right, a snake with an irresistible desire for cake. And this craving was about to land Sammy in a sticky, hilarious situation. One afternoon, as the smell of freshly baked goods wafted through the air, Sammy's snake senses perked up. He followed his nose, or rather his forked tongue, and stumbled upon the grand opening of his town's first-ever bakery. The display window was filled with an array of yummy cakes, each one more tempting than the last.

Unable to resist the temptation, Sammy slithered inside, his beady eyes fixed on the glorious cakes. The baker, a kind-hearted woman named Betty, glanced at the snake and chuckled, "Well, hello there, Sammy! Are you here for a slice of cake too?"

Sammy's forked tongue flicked out in excitement, his mouth watering at the thought of sinking his fangs into a sugary delight. Betty, thinking it was all in good fun, reached behind the counter and handed him a small slice of chocolate cake. "Enjoy, Sammy!" she said with a wink.

Without a moment's hesitation, Sammy engulfed the slice of cake in one swift gulp. But to his surprise, the cake didn't go down as smoothly as he had expected. It felt like a bowling ball had lodged itself in his snake belly. Imagine the sight! Sammy's eyes widened in panic as he realized he had swallowed the slice whole, forgetting that snakes were not built for such big bits of cake.

Unable to move and with a belly full of cake, Sammy found himself in a bit of a troublesome situation. He tried slithering, but he ended up rolling around like a roly-poly snake-shaped ball. The people in the bakery gasped and burst into laughter, watching the cake-filled snake tumble around in a hilarious way.

Word of Sammy's cake issues spread like wildfire, and soon the entire town was buzzing with laughter. People gathered from all corners of the town, armed with cameras and smartphones, ready to capture the sight of the snake who had bitten off more cake than he could chew.

Meanwhile, Betty, overcome with guilt, tried to help poor Sammy. She enlisted the help of the local vet, Dr. Hilarious, who specialized in snake-related emergencies. Dr. Hilarious arrived with his trusty snake-handling tools, his face red from suppressing his laughter. With great care, Dr. Hilarious attempted to extract the cake from Sammy's belly. He prodded and poked, trying to coax the cake out. But no matter how hard he tried, the cake seemed determined to stay put.

The townspeople watched the crazy situation. They chanted, "Cake! Cake! Cake!" as if cheering on a wrestler in the ring. The situation had turned into the town's greatest entertainment, and no one could resist joining in. Finally, after what felt like an eternity, a ray of hope emerged. Sammy let out an enormous belch, a sound that resonated throughout the town like a sonic boom. And just like that, the cake popped out, landing with a squishy thud on the floor.

The crowd erupted into applause, cheering for Sammy's newfound freedom. The snake, now relieved of his cake-induced bellyache, slithered away in embarrassment, vowing to stick to his natural diet of mice and insects.

THE LAMB WHO SAT IN A PRAM

While his woolly friends wondered in the meadows and nibbled on grass, Larry had a rather interesting hobby — he loved to sit in a pram. Yes, you heard that right, a lamb who preferred the comfort of a pram over the grassy fields. And this preference was about to lead Larry on a hilariously unexpected adventure.

It all began on a sunny spring morning, as the farm was buzzing with activity. The farmer's daughter, a little girl named Lucy, had just received a brand new pram as a gift. With bright pink wheels and a cozy cushioned seat, the pram was a sight to behold.

As Lucy eagerly pushed her pram around the farmyard, Larry's beady eyes widened with fascination. He couldn't resist the look of the plush cushioned seat, calling out to him like a fluffy cloud of comfort. Without a second thought, Larry hopped right into the pram, his tiny hooves perched on the seat.

Lucy turned around, her eyes widening with surprise. "Oh my, a lamb in my pram!" she exclaimed, her face lighting up with a mischievous grin. Instead of shooing Larry away, Lucy found the sight hilarious and decided to let him stay.

Word of the lamb in the pram spread like wildfire among the animals on the farm. They gathered around, their eyes wide with disbelief. The chickens clucked in confusion, the cows mooed in amusement, and even the pigs oinked with laughter.

Larry, now basking in his newfound fame, became the talk of the farm. He would sit in the pram as if he were the king of the farmyard. The other animals would gather around, watching with awe and admiration. "Look at Larry, the lamb who sat in a pram!" they would say, their voices filled with laughter.

But Larry's pram adventures didn't end there. One day, as Lucy was taking the pram for a walk around the farm, a gust of wind swept through the fields, carrying the pram away. Lucy, too small and too surprised to hold onto the pram, watched in horror as it rolled down a hill, with Larry still snugly seated inside. The farm animals gasped in shock, their eyes glued to the pram hurtling down the hill like a rollercoaster ride. The chickens flapped their wings, the cows stumbled in disbelief, and even the pigs oinked in a mix of concern and amusement.

Down the hill, the pram continued its wild journey, bouncing over rocks and twigs, with Larry holding on for dear life. His woolly coat flapped in the wind as the pram gained speed, creating a comical sight that had the farm animals in stitches.

Meanwhile, Larry's adventurous ride attracted the attention of the neighbouring farm, where a group of mischievous goats watched with wide-eyed curiosity. The goats, known for their daredevil antics, saw an opportunity for some excitement. They sprang into action, chasing after the runaway pram in hope they could catchup with Larry.

The pram like a runway train went fast through the neighbouring farm, with Larry still perched inside. The goats chased after it, their hooves clattering on the ground, creating chaos that echoed through the countryside. It was a comical chase that had everyone on the edge of their seats, or rather, their hooves.

Finally, as the pram reached the edge of a steep hill, the goats managed to catch up. They surrounded the pram, their mischievous grins giving way to worried expressions. With one mighty leap, the leader of the goats, aptly named Gustavo, hopped into the pram, adding his weight to balance its momentum.

The pram came to a screeching halt, teetering perilously on the edge of the ravine. The farm animals, who had followed the chase from a safe distance, let out a collective sigh of relief. Larry, still seated in the pram, blinked his innocent eyes, seemingly unaware of the thrilling ride he had just experienced.

Lucy, who had followed the commotion, rushed over to retrieve her pram and a slightly dazed but unharmed Larry. She hugged him tightly, grateful for the goats' intervention. "Oh, Larry, you're such an adventurous lamb!" she exclaimed, a mixture of worry and laughter in her voice.

And as for Larry, well, he continued to live his life with a touch of silliness and a knack for finding hilarity in the most unexpected situations. He remained the farm's beloved comedian and as the animals, said, "Larry the Lamb, the pram-riding star of the farmyard, always keeps us smiling, come what may!"

THE GOAT WHO LIVED IN A BOAT

While other goats roamed the hills and grazed on grass, Gary lived in a boat! Yes, you heard it right, a goat who called a boat his home. And this unusual living arrangement was about to lead Gary on a hilariously absurd adventure.

It all began when Gary stumbled upon an old abandoned boat washed ashore. The boat had weathered many storms, and its sails were tattered, but to Gary, it was love at first sight. He hopped right into the boat, his hooves tapping on the wooden deck, and made himself comfortable. Little did Gary know that he was about to embark on a comical nautical journey.

Word of Gary's unique living situation quickly spread throughout the world. People couldn't help but chuckle at the sight of a goat perched on a boat. They gathered along the shoreline, cameras in hand, waiting to catch a glimpse of this sea-faring goat in action as he travelled around the world.

Gary, blissfully unaware of the attention he was garnering, spent his days exploring the nooks and crannies of his boat, chewing on seaweed, and practicing his goat balancing act on the ship's mast. His hilarious antics turned him into a celebrity of the seaside.

On one afternoon as Gary was basking in the sun on the deck of his boat, he peered over the edge of the boat and saw a group of fishermen struggling to haul in their catch. Their nets were filled to the brim with lots of fish, and they were in desperate need of assistance.

Being the helpful and adventure-seeking goat that he was, Gary sprang into action. He leaped off his boat, making a splash as he landed in the water, and swam towards the fishermen. His hooves thrashed through the waves with a determination that would put Olympic swimmers to shame.
The fishermen couldn't believe their eyes. "A goat to the rescue!" they exclaimed, their laughter mingling with astonishment. With Gary's assistance, they were able to bring in their catch with ease.

The mayor, impressed by the goat's bravery, declared him an honorary member of the fishing community. Gary, now adorned with a tiny sailor's hat and a miniature captain's jacket, became the mascot of the town's fishing fleet.

But Gary's sea adventures were far from over. One evening, as he was peacefully dozing in his boat, a group of mischievous seagulls decided to pay him a visit. They perched on the mast, flapping their wings and squawking. Gary, being a goat who couldn't resist a good prank, decided to join in on the fun. With a twinkle in his eye, Gary leaped onto the mast, bouncing up and down with all his goatly might. The seagulls squawked with delight as they took flight, carried by the rhythmic motion of the goat's impromptu trampoline. It was a sight to behold — a goat and a flock of seagulls bouncing and soaring through the air in perfect harmony.

Gary's boat became the center of attention in the seaside town of where he had helped the fishermen. The town even held an annual festival in Gary's honour, where goats dressed as sailors and seagulls swooped through the air. Laughter filled the streets as locals and tourists came together to celebrate the joy and silliness that Gary had brought to their lives.

So, the next time you find yourself near a seaside town, keep an eye out for a boat with a goat perched on its deck. Appreciate the goat who reminded an entire town that sometimes, the most extraordinary tales can be found in the most unexpected places.

THE OWL WHO KNEW HOW TO HOWL

One starry evening, as Oliver perched on his favourite branch, he felt an irresistible urge to let out a howl. He opened his beak and emitted a long, melodious howl that resonated through the forest. It was a sound unlike any other, a combination of hoots and howls that echoed through the trees.

Little did Oliver know that his exceptional howling abilities had caught the attention of a group of woodland animals. Curiosity piqued, they ventured closer, their eyes wide with wonder. It was a sight to behold — an owl sitting atop a branch, howling as if he were part wolf.

Oliver, thrilled by the attention and eager to entertain, continued to howl to his heart's content. Each night, he would perch on his branch and let out a symphony of hoots and howls, accompanied by the laughter of his forest friends. The forest became alive with laughter, as creatures from all walks of life gathered to witness the owl's nightly performances.

But Oliver's howling prowess didn't stop there. He decided to take his talent on the road, or rather, through the forest. With a mischievous twinkle in his eyes, he embarked on a mission to teach the other animals in the forest how to howl.

Oliver first approached his dear friend, Freddie the Fox, who was known for his cunning and sly nature. "Freddie, my friend, would you like to learn how to howl?" Oliver asked, his feathers ruffled with excitement.

Freddie's eyes widened with curiosity. "Howl? Me? But I'm a fox, Oliver. We don't howl, we bark!" he exclaimed.

Oliver, undeterred, let out a howl that sent shivers down Freddie's spine. "Nonsense, my foxy friend! Howling is for everyone, not just the wolves. Let me show you the art of the howl!"

And so, Oliver taught Freddie the art of howling. They practiced together, with Freddie attempting to imitate Oliver's melodious howls. The forest reverberated with laughter as Freddie's barks turned into a mixture of howls and hoots. It was a sight that left the other animals in stitches.

Next, Oliver approached Lola the Hedgehog, known for her prickly demeanour. "Lola, my spiky friend, would you like to learn the art of the howl?" Oliver asked, his eyes twinkling with mischief.

Lola rolled into a tight ball, her quills standing on end. "A hedgehog howling? Now I've heard everything!" she snorted.

Undeterred by Lola's doubt, Oliver demonstrated his howling prowess. He unleashed a series of hoots and howls that made Lola's quills stand on end. "You see, Lola, howling is for creatures big and small, prickly or not. Let's give it a try!"

And so, Oliver and Lola practiced together, their howls and snorts mingling in the moonlit night. The forest was filled with laughter as Lola's quills quivered with each attempt. It was a comical sight that had the other animals in stitches.

One night, as Oliver was teaching a chorus of frogs how to howl, a gust of wind swept through the forest, carrying his melodious howls far and wide. The sound travelled to a nearby circus, where a troupe of performing animals were preparing for their grand show.

The circus animals, from the daring lion to the graceful elephant, paused in their tracks, mesmerized by the sound. They had never heard such a captivating howl, and it piqued their curiosity.

The circus director, a flamboyant ringmaster named Mr. Pizzazz, was known for his love of spectacle. He knew that this unique talent could be the highlight of their upcoming show.

He approached the forest, guided by the sound of Oliver's howls. As he arrived, the animals fell silent, their eyes wide with anticipation. Mr. Pizzazz looked at Oliver, his eyes gleaming with excitement. "My dear owl, would you like to bring your howling talent to the grandest stage of all?"

Oliver's feathers fluffed up with delight. This was an opportunity he couldn't resist. He accepted Mr. Pizzazz's offer and joined the circus troupe, ready to showcase his extraordinary howling skills to the world.

And so, the night of the grand show arrived. The circus was packed with an audience eager to witness the spectacle. As the spotlight shone on Oliver, he took a deep breath and let out a howl that reverberated through the tent.

The audience gasped in awe, their eyes fixed on the owl on center stage. Oliver's howls combined with the laughter of the forest animals, creating a symphony of joy that echoed through the circus.

From that moment on, Oliver became the star of the circus, captivating audiences with his unique talent. He taught the other circus animals the art of howling, creating a show unlike any other. The circus became a place of laughter and delight, where animals of all shapes and sizes embraced their inner howlers.

THE MASSIVE MOOSE THAT WAS LET LOOSE

Once upon a time, in the heart of a vast forest, there lived a massive moose named Marvin, he was not your average moose. While other moose roamed the woods with grace and poise, Marvin had a knack for getting into hilarious predicaments. And this comical nature was about to lead Marvin on an adventure that would leave the forest in stitches.

It all began one sunny morning when Marvin woke up feeling mischievous. He decided it was time to break free from his usual routine and let loose, quite literally. With a mighty kick of his powerful hooves, Marvin burst through the wooden fence that surrounded his favourite grazing spot. He felt an exhilarating rush as he galloped through the forest, his antlers held high, and his massive body bounding with enthusiasm.

Word of the massive moose on the loose spread like wildfire among the woodland creatures. Squirrels chattered excitedly, birds whistled with astonishment, and even the wise old owl hooted with laughter. They couldn't believe their eyes — a colossal moose rampaging through the forest, leaving chaos and laughter in his wake.

Marvin, fuelled by the attention and laughter, continued his wild adventure. He darted through the trees, narrowly missing branches and bushes, his antlers becoming entangled in leaves and twigs. It was a sight to behold, a moose-shaped whirlwind of laughter and chaos that had the entire forest on edge.

But little did Marvin know that his escapades had caught the attention of the bumbling duo, Benny and Barney, two aspiring wildlife photographers. These two hapless friends, armed with cameras and an insatiable thirst for adventure, were always on the lookout for the next big shot.

When Benny and Barney heard about the massive moose on the loose, their eyes lit up with excitement. They knew this was their chance to capture the photo of a lifetime. With cameras slung around their necks, they set off into the forest, ready to document Marvin's hilarious journey.

As Marvin bounded through the forest, his massive hooves stomping with each step, he stumbled upon a picturesque meadow. A brilliant idea sparked in his moose-sized brain — he decided to put on a show for his newfound fans. With a theatrical flair, Marvin leaped into the air, twirled around, and performed a perfect pirouette.

Benny and Barney, who had been cautiously following Marvin's trail, gasped in awe as they witnessed the massive moose's acrobatic display. They fumbled with their cameras, desperately trying to capture the extraordinary moment. But in their excitement, Benny tripped over a root, and Barney's camera slipped from his hands, crashing into the ground with a resounding thud.

The forest erupted with laughter, as Benny and Barney joined in on the comedy of errors. Marvin, unaware of the chaos he had caused, continued his performance, twirling and prancing as the forest creatures cheered him on.

The sight of Benny and Barney's clumsy attempts at photography, mixed with Marvin's majestic yet comical dance, had the animals rolling on the ground, tears streaming down their furry cheeks. The forest became a symphony of laughter, with Marvin as the star of the show.

But as the laughter subsided, Marvin sensed something was amiss. He stopped his performance and turned to face Benny and Barney, who were dusting themselves off and grinning sheepishly. Realizing the chaos they had inadvertently caused, Benny and Barney approached Marvin with apologetic expressions.

"We're so sorry, Marvin!" Benny exclaimed, his face flushed with embarrassment. "We didn't mean to disrupt your show. We were just trying to capture the moment, and things got a little out of hand."

Barney nodded in agreement, a sheepish grin on his face. "Yeah, Marvin, we got carried away with the excitement. We hope you're not too mad at us!"

Marvin's eyes twinkled with amusement as he looked at the duo. He realized that their clumsiness had inadvertently added an extra dose of laughter to his escapades. With a shake of his antlers, Marvin forgave Benny and Barney, accepting their presence as part of his ongoing comedy routine.

From that day on, Benny and Barney became Marvin's official sidekicks, documenting his misadventures with their cameras. The trio traversed the forest, leaving laughter and chaos in their wake. The animals eagerly awaited Marvin's next act, always ready to join in the mirthful chorus of laughter.

And so, the massive moose who was let loose, along with his bumbling companions, became a legend in the forest. The tale of their hilarious escapades echoed through the trees, bringing joy to animals far and wide.

Marvin taught the woodland creatures that laughter is the best medicine, even in the face of chaos and unexpected events. He showed them that sometimes, letting loose and embracing the absurdity of life can lead to the most unforgettable and laughter-filled adventures.

THE ARMADILLO THAT SAT ON A PILLOW

Every day, like clockwork, Arthur would search the land for the perfect pillow to sit on. It had to be just the right fluffiness, with a touch of elegance, and a hint of charm. Once he found the ideal pillow, he would curl up on it, feeling the softness embrace his armoured shell. Arthur believed that life was simply too short to sit on anything less than the comfiest of cushions.

One afternoon, as Arthur waddled through the forest, he stumbled upon a grand pillow department store. His eyes widened with delight, for there before him lay a multitude of pillows, each one more alluring than the last. There were silky pillows, fluffy pillows, and even pillows with intricate patterns and designs.

Unable to contain his excitement, Arthur darted inside the store, his tiny armadillo legs propelling him forward. The store owner, a plump raccoon named Reginald, greeted him with a knowing smile.

"Ah, Arthur! I see you've come to find the perfect pillow once again," Reginald said, his eyes twinkling with mirth.

"You know me too well, Reginald," Arthur replied with a chuckle. "I'm on a never-ending quest for ultimate comfort!"

Together, they walked the aisles, inspecting pillows of every shape and size. Arthur ran his paws along the velvety surfaces, feeling the textures tickle his sensitive armadillo snout.

Finally, at the back of the store, Arthur spotted a pillow that made his heart skip a beat. It was the softest, fluffiest pillow he had ever laid eyes upon, adorned with shimmering stars.

"I must have it!" Arthur exclaimed; his eyes gleaming with excitement.

Reginald, unable to resist Arthur's infectious enthusiasm, placed the pillow in Arthur's tiny armadillo arms. "It's the perfect match for you, my friend. May it bring you endless comfort and joy."

With his new prized possession in tow, Arthur bid farewell to Reginald and scurried back to his cozy burrow. He carefully arranged the starry pillow in the center, fluffing it with great care. Arthur then plopped himself onto his newfound throne, his armoured shell sinking into the plushness.

On day as he lounged on his pillow, a gentle breeze whisked through the trees, carrying the sweet aroma of freshly baked cookies wafting through the forest.

Intrigued, Arthur followed his nose, his tiny armadillo feet guiding him towards the source of the heavenly smell. He emerged from the undergrowth to find a lively baking contest taking place, with animals from all walks of life competing for the title of Forest's Best Baker.

Arthur's eyes sparkled with excitement. "I may not be a baker," he thought, "but perhaps my pillow can inspire a creation that will tickle the taste buds!"

With the starry pillow nestled under his arm, Arthur approached the contest judges, a panel of distinguished forest dwellers.

"Good sirs and madams, I present to you my creation—Pillow Puffs!" Arthur declared, lifting the corner of his pillow to reveal a tray of delectable pastries. The onlookers gasped, their eyes widening in curiosity.

The judges, intrigued by this unique offering, bit into the Pillow Puffs, and their taste buds were greeted by a burst of flavour and an indescribable feeling of comfort. The pastries melted in their mouths, leaving them craving more.

The forest erupted in applause as Arthur's Pillow Puffs were declared the winning creation. The animals cheered, their laughter filling the air as they savoured the unique blend of deliciousness and cozy comfort.

From that day on, Arthur became known as the armadillo with the magic pillow and the knack for creating the most delightful treats. The forest animals eagerly awaited his next culinary invention, knowing that each bite would be an experience like no other.

THE STORK WHO ATE A FORK

It all began on a sunny day as Stanley soared through the sky, his long wings flapping with elegance. He was on a routine delivery, carrying a precious bundle of joy in his beak, when a gust of wind startled him. In a moment of panic, Stanley opened his beak wide, and to his surprise, a nearby picnic-goer's fork flew straight into his throat.

Stanley gagged and squawked, flapping his wings in a frenzy. The fork was stuck, and try as he might, Stanley couldn't dislodge it. Panic settled in as he struggled to breathe properly. The townsfolk below, initially confused by the sight of a fork-wielding stork, soon realized the gravity of the situation.

"Quick! We must help poor Stanley!" cried Mrs. Puddlefoot, the wise old duck who lived by the river. The townsfolk gathered around, brainstorming ideas to free Stanley from his fork-induced predicament.

After several failed attempts involving fishing rods, lassos, and even a makeshift crane, they came to a sudden realization—a solution had been staring them in the face all along. It was none other than Dr. Featherbottom, the renowned avian veterinarian.

Dr. Featherbottom, a dapper owl with a knack for solving unusual ailments, arrived in a flurry of feathers. He assessed Stanley's condition with a wise nod, his spectacles perched precariously on his beak. After a brief examination, he proposed an unconventional but potentially effective remedy.

"Stanley, my feathered friend, we shall attempt a ticklish intervention," Dr. Featherbottom declared, a twinkle in his eye. "We shall make you laugh so hard that the fork pops right out!"

The people around exchanged glances, unsure if this plan was truly wise. But with no other viable options on the table, they decided to trust Dr. Featherbottom's unconventional approach.

The people around scurried around, gathering feathers, rubber chickens, and all manner of ticklish objects. They formed a circle around Stanley, their faces filled with determination. With synchronized precision, they tickled, prodded, and poked the poor stork, hoping to elicit a fit of uncontrollable laughter.

Stanley squirmed and flapped his wings, trying to resist the tickling onslaught. But the townsfolk were persistent, their fingers dancing along his feathers. Laughter erupted from Stanley's beak, a mixture of squawks and chuckles that echoed through the town square.

Suddenly, as if by magic, the fork flew out of Stanley's throat and landed with a clatter on the ground. The people erupted in cheers, their laughter mingling with joyous relief. Stanley, free from his fork-induced ailment, joined in the mirthful celebration, flapping his wings and twirling with glee.

News of his unconventional remedy reached the ears of a renowned filmmaker, Mr. Featherstone, who was famous for his quirky and offbeat documentaries. Intrigued by Stanley's story, Mr. Featherstone set out to capture the stork's misadventures on film.

With cameras and crew in tow, Mr. Featherstone arrived in Featherbrook, ready to document Stanley's journey. They followed Stanley as he went about his daily stork duties, from delivering bundles of joy to dancing in the rain. The townsfolk, now accustomed to the presence of cameras, embraced the opportunity to showcase their unique town and its feathered hero.

The film, titled "The Fork and the Feather," became an instant sensation. Audiences around the world laughed and marvelled at Stanley's peculiar escapade. They were inspired by his resilience, charmed by his sense of humour, and moved by the unity and determination of the townsfolk.

Stanley, now a celebrity in his own right, embraced his newfound fame with a beaming smile. He attended movie premieres, posed for photoshoots, and even learned a few dance moves from a troupe of tap-dancing penguins. Life had taken an unexpected turn, and Stanley was determined to make the most of it.

Stanley never forgot his humble beginnings. He continued to soar through the skies, delivering bundles of joy with a newfound grace and a mischievous twinkle in his eye. He would occasionally stumble upon a discarded fork, and with a playful flick of his beak, he would send it flying through the air, reminding himself and the townsfolk of the hilarious adventure that had changed their lives forever, for laughter has the power to transform even the most peculiar moments into cherished memories.

THE FLY WHO GOT LOST IN SKY

Freddy the fly had big dreams of exploring the wide-open sky. But little did he know, his pursuit of adventure would lead to a comical and unforgettable journey.

One sunny morning, as Freddy fluttered about, he noticed a beautiful hot air balloon floating gracefully in the sky. The vibrant colours and the sense of freedom it represented mesmerized him. He couldn't resist the urge to join in on the airborne fun.

With a burst of excitement, Freddy zipped towards the hot air balloon, ready to hitch a ride and embark on his grand adventure. As he approached the balloon, a gust of wind caught him by surprise, whisking him away into the vast expanse of the sky.

Freddy's tiny wings flapped furiously as he struggled to keep up with the balloon. But try as he might, he couldn't keep pace. Before he knew it, the hot air balloon drifted further and further away, leaving Freddy all alone in the wide-open sky.

Panicked but determined, Freddy looked around, hoping to spot a familiar landmark. But all he saw was an endless blue canopy above and the sprawling landscape far below. He was lost in the sky.

As Freddy's wings grew tired, he spotted a group of geese flying in a V-formation. Hopeful that they might lead him back home, he decided to follow them. With each flap of their powerful wings, the geese soared effortlessly through the sky, their honking cheers echoing through the air.

Freddy, being much smaller and less aerodynamic than the geese, struggled to keep up. He bobbed and weaved, narrowly avoiding collisions with his larger feathered friends. Despite his valiant efforts, he couldn't maintain the speed and eventually lost sight of the geese.

Now completely disoriented, Freddy found himself in the company of a group of skydivers. They were soaring through the air, their colourful parachutes billowing in the wind. Freddy thought this might be his chance to find his way back home.

Filled with determination, Freddy glided down towards the skydivers, hoping they could guide him to safety. But as he approached, he realized that these daredevils had no intention of helping him. They mistook him for a pesky bug and began swatting at him, sending Freddy spiralling out of control.

Downward he plummeted, his tiny wings flapping frantically as he struggled to regain control. With a stroke of luck, he landed safely on the billowing parachute of an unsuspecting skydiver named Dave.

Dave, oblivious to the little stowaway on his parachute, descended gently to the ground. As soon as he touched down, Freddy buzzed away, grateful for his narrow escape. He was determined to find his way back to Flutterville, even if it meant facing more challenges along the way.

As Freddy explored his surroundings, he stumbled upon a group of kites soaring high in the sky. Excited by their colourful presence, he fluttered towards them, hoping they could help guide him home. But, as luck would have it, one mischievous kite named Kip had other plans.

Kip, a playful and mischievous kite, loved to tease and play pranks. Spotting Freddy, he couldn't resist the opportunity for some airborne fun. With a swift motion, Kip swooped down and grabbed Freddy's tiny leg, taking him on an unexpected joyride.

Freddy's eyes widened with surprise as he soared through the sky, tethered to the mischievous kite. Up, down, and all around they went, performing aerial acrobatics that left Freddy dizzy and disoriented. He called out for help, but his voice was carried away by the wind.

Eventually, after what seemed like an eternity, Kip released his grip, sending Freddy tumbling through the air. Disoriented and dizzy, Freddy fluttered towards a passing flock of seagulls, hoping they could guide him back home.

The seagulls, known for their love of mischief and scavenging, noticed Freddy's messy state. Intrigued by the little fly, they decided to have some fun. They darted and swooped, trying to catch Freddy in their beaks, thinking he would make a tasty snack.

Freddy dodged and weaved, narrowly escaping the clutches of the seagulls. He was determined to find his way back to Flutterville, and he wouldn't let a flock of mischievous seagulls deter him.

With newfound resolve, Freddy mustered his remaining energy and flew higher into the sky. As he soared above the clouds, he caught sight of a familiar landmark—a tall tree standing proudly in the distance. It was the very same tree he had left behind in Flutterville.

Filled with joy and relief, Freddy followed his instincts, navigating through the sky until he landed safely back in his beloved town. The familiar sights and sounds welcomed him, and the townsfolk rejoiced at his safe return.

As Freddy shared his incredible journey with his friends, they listened in awe. They marvelled at his bravery and laughed at the comical encounters he had faced. Freddy had become a hero in their eyes—a fly who had dared to explore the vast sky.

THE PIG WHO WORE A WIG

On a charming little farm nestled in the countryside, there lived a pig named Percy. While the other pigs were content rolling in the mud and munching on slop, Percy had a peculiar obsession—he loved fashion! And one day, his quest for style led him on a hilarious adventure that would leave the farm in stitches.

It all began on a sunny morning when Percy waddled over to the farm's scarecrow, Scarecrow Steve, who was diligently guarding the crops. Percy admired the straw hat perched atop Steve's head and thought, "Hmm, why should scarecrows have all the fashion fun?"

With a mischievous glint in his eye, Percy hatched a plan. He set off to explore the farm in search of the perfect accessory to elevate his own style. After rummaging through the farmer's shed and digging through a forgotten trunk, Percy stumbled upon a magnificent wig.

The wig was curly and pink, with cascading waves that seemed to dance in the breeze. Percy's heart raced with excitement. He couldn't resist the allure of this fabulous hairpiece. With a swift movement, he placed the wig on his head and stood tall, admiring his new look in the mirror.

Oh, how Percy felt transformed! He strutted around the farmyard, tossing his head from side to side, his wig swaying in rhythm. The other animals, caught off guard by Percy's newfound glamour, couldn't help but chuckle at the sight of a pig parading in a pink wig.

Henry, the wise old horse, approached Percy with a knowing smile. "Percy, my friend, you certainly know how to make a statement! But be careful, as wigs can be quite unpredictable."

Percy dismissed Henry's warning with a snort. He was too captivated by his stylish appearance to consider any potential consequences. With a flip of his wig-adorned snout, Percy marched onward, determined to show off his fashionable flair.

As Percy made his way through the farm, word of his audacious style spread among the animals. The cows mooed in amusement, the chickens clucked with delight, and even the sheep couldn't help but giggle at the sight of Percy's pink wig.

But Percy's fashion-forward choices caught the attention of someone unexpected—Greta, the farm's resident fashionista goose. Greta, known for her impeccable taste and flair for the dramatic, was intrigued by Percy's audacity.

With her feathers ruffled in excitement, Greta approached Percy, her beady eyes twinkling. "Oh, darling Percy, your wig is simply marvellous! But if you truly want to make a fashion statement, you must join me at the annual Barnyard Fashion Extravaganza!"

Percy's eyes widened with excitement. The Barnyard Fashion Extravaganza was a legendary event, where animals from far and wide showcased their most daring and innovative styles. Percy couldn't believe his luck—he had a chance to become a farmyard fashion icon!

With Greta by his side, Percy set off on a whirlwind adventure, preparing for the extravagant event. They rummaged through the farmer's discarded clothes, experimenting with feather boas, oversized sunglasses, and even a pair of glittery cowboy boots. The farmyard became their fashion laboratory, buzzing with creativity and laughter.

The day of the Barnyard Fashion Extravaganza arrived, and the farm was abuzz with excitement. Animals of all shapes and sizes gathered in anticipation, eagerly awaiting the grand unveiling of Percy's showstopping look.

As Percy sashayed onto the runway, his pink wig shimmering in the sunlight, gasps of astonishment filled the air. The audience was mesmerized by his confidence and unique style. Chickens clapped their wings in approval, cows swished their tails, and the sheep bleated in sheer delight.

But as Percy strutted his stuff, his wig decided to take matters into its own curly hands. It started to slide down Percy's head, threatening to cover his eyes. Percy, caught off guard, attempted to adjust the wig with a quick shake of his head, but it only worsened the situation.

The wig slipped further, obscuring Percy's vision entirely. Panic set in as Percy wiggled and jiggled, desperately trying to free himself from the clutches of the rogue hairpiece. His attempts at liberation only made matters worse, sending the wig flying through the air like a pink tornado.

The farmyard erupted in laughter as Percy twirled and spun, his wig soaring above him. It landed on the head of Scarecrow Steve, who suddenly found himself transformed into the most fashionable scarecrow in all the land.

The sight of a scarecrow donning a pink curly wig was too much for the animals to handle. They doubled over with laughter, tears streaming down their faces. Even Greta, who prided herself on her refined taste, couldn't help but join in the hilarity of the moment.

THE SNAIL WHO DELIVERED MAIL

Other snails were content with their slow-paced lives, Stanley had big dreams of becoming the village mail carrier. Little did he know, his ambition would lead to a comical adventure filled with laughter and surprises. One day as Stanley slithered along at his usual snail's pace, he noticed a group of villagers bustling around the post office. Letters and packages were piling up, and the village desperately needed a mail carrier. Stanley's eyes widened with excitement. This was his chance to shine!

With a determined smile, Stanley approached the postmaster, Mr. Johnson, and volunteered his services. Mr. Johnson, who was known for his patience, chuckled and said, "Stanley, my friend, being a mail carrier requires a certain level of speed and efficiency. But I admire your enthusiasm. Why don't we give it a try?" Stanley's heart skipped a beat as he was handed a small bag full of letters. It was time for his very first mail delivery. The villagers, curious and amused, gathered around to witness this slow-speed adventure.

With his shell proudly polished and his eyes sparkling with excitement, Stanley set off on his delivery route. The villagers watched in anticipation, wondering just how long it would take for their letters to arrive.

As Stanley inched along, the villagers quickly realized that this was not going to be an ordinary mail delivery. They gathered chairs and snacks, preparing for what would undoubtedly be an entertaining and leisurely afternoon. Meanwhile, in his own snail-paced world, Stanley hummed a cheerful tune as he carefully read each address on the envelopes. The first letter was for Old Mrs. Puddlefoot, who lived at the end of a winding path. Stanley smiled and began his slow but steady journey.

As Stanley approached Mrs. Puddlefoot's house, he spotted a juicy lettuce leaf on the ground. Unable to resist its tempting aroma, he paused for a delightful snack. Little did he know, this momentary detour would turn into a hilarious scene.

Mrs. Puddlefoot, peering out her window, noticed the snail making himself at home in her front yard. Her eyes widened with astonishment. "Why, it seems I have a snail enjoying a feast in my garden! How delightful!"

With a twinkle in her eye, Mrs. Puddlefoot decided to join in the fun. She fetched her own chair, placed it beside Stanley, and cheerfully began a conversation with her new snail friend.

As the villagers gathered around, they burst into laughter at the sight of Mrs. Puddlefoot engaged in lively conversation with the snail. It seemed that Stanley's mail delivery had unintentionally become a social event, complete with refreshments and delightful company.

After what felt like an eternity, Stanley bid Mrs. Puddlefoot farewell and continued on his delivery route. The villagers, their laughter still echoing in the air, eagerly awaited the next stop on Stanley's mail delivery adventure.

The next letter was for the mischievous twins, Jack and Jill. Their house was perched atop a small hill, which required Stanley to navigate a winding path. The villagers settled in, knowing that this delivery would surely provide more hilarity and laughter.

As Stanley slowly ascended the hill, Jack and Jill spotted him from their bedroom window. They gasped in astonishment, their eyes widening with mischief. This was an opportunity they couldn't resist.

The mischievous twins hatched a plan. They ran outside, carefully placing obstacles in Stanley's path. They set up tiny hurdles made of twigs and sprinkled their toys along the way. Their intention was to create an amusing obstacle course for the slow and steady mail carrier.

Stanley, blissfully unaware of the twins' mischief, approached the hill with determination. But as he encountered each hurdle, he faced a delightful challenge. His shell bumped against twigs, and his path was filled with playful surprises.

The villagers, who had gathered at the bottom of the hill, cheered Stanley on, their laughter filling the air. With each hurdle he crossed, the atmosphere grew livelier and more joyous. Even the mischievous twins couldn't help but giggle at Stanley's unwavering determination.

After what seemed like an eternity, Stanley finally reached the top of the hill. Jack and Jill were waiting with wide grins, eager to greet their slow but steadfast mail carrier. They thanked him with a playful pat on his shell and bid him farewell.

As Stanley continued his mail delivery, the villagers eagerly awaited his next stop. Each letter he delivered became an occasion for laughter, amusement, and shared moments of delight. The village had transformed into a vibrant community bonded by laughter and the joy of Stanley's unique mail delivery style.

As Stanley reached his final destination, the whole village erupted in applause. The villagers gathered around, praising Stanley for his dedication and creating unforgettable memories. Mr. Johnson, the postmaster, chuckled and admitted that Stanley's slow but sincere approach to mail delivery had brought an unexpected joy to the village.

Stanley, he continued his mail delivery duties, taking his time and savouring every moment. He understood that sometimes, it's not the speed that matters, but the journey itself—the moments of connection, laughter, and unexpected friendships that make life truly special.

THE DEER WITH ONLY ONE EAR

In a peaceful forest filled with towering trees and lush greenery, there lived a deer named Douglas. While other deer roamed the forest with their majestic antlers, Douglas had a rather peculiar characteristic—he had only one ear! But little did he know, his unique appearance would lead to a hilarious and unforgettable adventure.

Douglas was proud of his single ear and wore it like a badge of honour. He would often strut around the forest, flaunting his unique trait. His fellow forest dwellers, though initially puzzled by his distinctive feature, soon grew fond of him and accepted him just the way he was.

As Douglas grazed near a sparkling stream, he overheard a group of squirrels chattering excitedly about a legendary treasure hidden deep within the forest. Their stories were filled with tales of sparkling gems, shimmering gold, and endless riches.

Intrigued by the idea of adventure and treasure, Douglas decided to embark on a quest to find this fabled treasure. He was convinced that his single ear would be an advantage, as it allowed him to hear things that others might miss. With his head held high, he set off on his grand expedition.

As Douglas ventured deeper into the forest, he encountered various challenges and met an array of eccentric characters. First, he stumbled upon a wise old owl named Oliver, perched high atop a tree branch.

"Hello, wise owl! I'm on a quest to find the legendary treasure hidden in this forest. Can you offer any guidance?" Douglas inquired, his eyes wide with excitement.

Oliver, with a knowing smile, nodded and replied, "Ah, the legendary treasure. Many have sought it, but few have succeeded. Remember, Douglas, treasure comes in many forms, not just gold and gems. Keep your heart open, and the true treasures of life will reveal themselves."

Douglas, grateful for Oliver's advice, continued his journey, his single ear twitching with anticipation. Along the way, he encountered a mischievous rabbit named Rosie, who offered to join him on his adventure.

"Hey there, Douglas! I've heard about the legendary treasure too! Let's team up and find it together," Rosie suggested, wiggling her nose mischievously.

Douglas, delighted by the company, gladly accepted Rosie's offer. With their unique traits, the duo made an unconventional but lovable team. They hopped and trotted through the forest, sharing laughs and funny stories along the way.

As they delved deeper into the forest, Douglas and Rosie stumbled upon a peculiar group of animals—a singing squirrel, a tap-dancing bear, and a beatboxing raccoon. These talented critters had formed a merry band called "The Funky Forest Crew."

Intrigued by their lively tunes and energetic performances, Douglas and Rosie couldn't resist joining the crew. With his single ear, Douglas added a unique rhythm to their beats, while Rosie's quick feet brought an extra dose of pizzazz to their dance routines.

The Funky Forest Crew, impressed by Douglas and Rosie's contributions, offered to help them on their quest for the legendary treasure. With their newfound friends, the duo felt invincible and ready to face any challenge that came their way.

But as luck would have it, their path was blocked by a rickety old bridge suspended over a treacherous river. The bridge looked as if it would crumble at the slightest touch.

Douglas, with his sharp senses, heard a faint whisper carried by the wind. It was the voice of the river itself, urging them to solve a riddle before crossing.

"Listen carefully, adventurers," the river murmured. "To cross this bridge and continue your quest, answer me this: What has a heart that doesn't beat?"

Douglas pondered the riddle, his single ear attuned to every sound. Suddenly, a giggle erupted from Rosie, who exclaimed, "A deck of cards! It has a heart, but it doesn't beat!"

The river rumbled in approval, and with a flick of its waves, the rickety bridge transformed into a sturdy path. The adventurers, grateful for their quick thinking, crossed the bridge and continued their journey.

As they pressed on, their path led them to a grove of trees, where a wise old tortoise named Timothy resided. Timothy had seen many wonders and possessed vast knowledge of the forest's secrets.

"Ah, young adventurers, seeking the legendary treasure, are you?" Timothy said with a knowing smile. "But remember, treasure is not solely found in wealth. It can be found in the friendships you make, the laughter you share, and the joy of the journey itself."

Douglas and Rosie nodded, their hearts filled with gratitude for Timothy's wise words. They understood that the true treasure was not just material wealth, but the experiences and memories they had gathered along the way.

Finally, after overcoming numerous challenges and laughter-filled moments, Douglas and Rosie arrived at a serene clearing. Bathed in golden sunlight, they discovered a magnificent tree with branches adorned with sparkling crystals—a sight that took their breath away.

"This must be the legendary treasure!" Douglas exclaimed, his single ear perked up in awe.

But as they approached, the tree began to shimmer and transform into something unexpected—a mesmerizing display of lights, colours, and enchanting melodies. It was nature's own treasure, a breathtaking spectacle that left the duo in awe.

They shared their tales of adventure and laughter, inspiring others to embark on their own journeys of discovery.

THE PARROTT WHO TURNED INTO A CARROT

Polly found herself perched on a branch, admiring the vibrant flowers in the nearby garden. Unbeknownst to her, a mischievous fairy named Fizzlebottom was practicing her spells nearby. Fizzlebottom, notorious for her shaky wand-wielding skills, accidentally let loose a burst of magical energy that zapped Polly right in the feathers.

In an instant, Polly felt a peculiar tingling sensation. She flapped her wings, expecting to take flight, but to her surprise, she couldn't move. Instead, she looked down to find her feathers turning a bright shade of orange, and her wings transformed into feathery green leaves. Polly had become a talking carrot!

With a bewildered squawk, Polly hopped off the branch, only to realize she couldn't hop very far. She rolled down a gentle slope and plopped into a vegetable patch, surrounded by an assortment of chatty radishes, talking tomatoes, and a rather opinionated cucumber named Cuthbert.

Cuthbert, noticing Polly's arrival, raised an eyebrow—or at least he would have if cucumbers had eyebrows. "Well, well, well. Look what we have here—a talking carrot. Welcome to the club," Cuthbert remarked, his voice dripping with sarcasm.

Polly, now a carrot, felt a mixture of surprise, confusion, and a hint of embarrassment. "I... I don't understand what happened. How did I end up like this?"

Cuthbert, rolling his cucumber eyes, sighed dramatically. "Oh, don't worry, my leafy friend. This is just one of Fizzlebottom's magical mishaps. She's notorious for turning things topsy-turvy. But fear not! I'm here to guide you through your carrot-y adventures."

And so, Polly, the parrot-turned-carrot, began her hilarious journey in the vegetable patch. With Cuthbert as her mentor, she learned the ins and outs of carrot life, discovering the joys and pitfalls of being a chatty root vegetable.

As Polly and Cuthbert discussed the latest gossip in the garden, they overheard a conversation nearby. It was the garden's wise old owl, Ollie, hooting with laughter.

"What's so funny, Ollie?" Cuthbert asked, his cucumber vine curling with curiosity.

Ollie, his eyes twinkling with amusement, hooted, "You won't believe what I just witnessed! Mrs. McGregor's naughty dog, Baxter, mistook a pile of talking carrots for a group of chatty squirrels. He was so confused, he spent the whole day trying to engage them in conversation!"

Polly, now a carrot, giggled uncontrollably. The image of a dog chatting with a bunch of carrots was simply too absurd to resist.

Inspired by this hilarious tale, Polly hatched a plan to bring laughter to the garden. She gathered her fellow talking vegetables and orchestrated a carrot chorus. As Baxter, the dog, trotted by the garden, Polly and her carrot comrades began chattering and singing in unison.

Baxter's ears perked up in surprise as he halted in his tracks. He couldn't believe his ears—or rather, his eyes—seeing a group of carrots moving and making noise. His tail wagged furiously as he approached the chatty carrots, ready for what he thought would be the conversation of a lifetime.

With her leafy green "arms" flailing, Polly initiated a lively carrot conversation with Baxter. Though no one else could understand the carrots' words, the scene was utterly comical—a dog earnestly barking at a bunch of animated carrots.

The garden burst into laughter as Polly and her fellow talking carrots engaged Baxter in a friendly chat. They discussed the weather, shared their favourite carrot recipes, and even gave Baxter some gardening advice. Baxter, though puzzled, wagged his tail happily, blissfully unaware that the carrots were, in fact, his vegetable friends.

As the sun set and laughter filled the garden, Fizzlebottom, the mischievous fairy responsible for Polly's carrot transformation, happened upon the uproarious scene. She gasped in surprise, her wand wobbling in her hand.

"Oh dear! It seems my magic went awry once again," Fizzlebottom exclaimed, her cheeks flushing with embarrassment.

Polly, now fully embracing her carrot form, hopped toward Fizzlebottom with a bright orange smile. "Don't worry, Fizzlebottom. You've given us a new perspective on life, quite literally. We've discovered the joy of laughter and friendship in our vegetable community."

Fizzlebottom, touched by Polly's acceptance, nodded gratefully. With a wave of her wand, she reversed the magic, restoring Polly to her vibrant parrot self.

As Polly fluttered her wings in delight, she glanced at her carrot friends, who had returned to their usual state. "Thank you all for your friendship and laughter. You've shown me that no matter our form, we can find joy and humour in the most unexpected situations."

The garden erupted in applause as the vegetables rejoiced, their leaves rustling with excitement. Polly, now back to her feathery self, bid farewell to her carrot companions but promised to visit them often.

Polly continued to embrace her mischievous nature and shared her hilarious tales with the other animals of Sunnyvale.

THE CHICKEN WHO WAS ALWAYS LICKIN

Whether it was a fence post, a patch of grass, or even the farmer's boots, Charlie couldn't resist giving things a good lick. Little did he know, his constant need to taste everything would lead to a hilarious adventure that would leave the farm in stitches.

It all began on a bright morning when Charlie woke up feeling a bit more adventurous than usual. As he strutted around the farmyard, he spotted something shiny glinting in the distance. It was a can of brightly coloured paint left behind by the farmer.

Curiosity got the better of Charlie, and before he knew it, his tongue was darting out, giving the can a lick. The taste of paint sent an unexpected tingling sensation through his beak. Charlie's eyes widened with excitement. He had discovered a new and thrilling hobby—lickin' paint!

Charlie couldn't resist the urge to lick anything with a splash of colour. He licked the red tractor, the blue barn door, and even the yellow sunflowers in the field. The other animals on the farm watched with amusement, chuckling at Charlie's eccentric behaviour. One day, as Charlie wandered near the farmer's house, he spotted a bright red mailbox. The mailbox looked absolutely lickable, and Charlie's beak watered with anticipation. He couldn't resist the temptation.

With a quick dart of his tongue, Charlie licked the mailbox. But to his surprise, instead of a burst of flavour, he received a jolt of electricity that made his feathers stand on end. The mailbox was wired to the farmer's security system!

Charlie flapped his wings in panic, desperately trying to free his beak from the electrified mailbox. With a final squawk, he managed to break free, but not without leaving a funny chicken-shaped mark on the mailbox.

The farmer, hearing the commotion, rushed out of the house to investigate. When he saw Charlie with his ruffled feathers and the humorous imprint on the mailbox, he burst into laughter. "Well, well, Charlie! Looks like you've left your mark on the farm!"

One by one, Charlie licked a yellow wheelbarrow, turning it green; he licked a brown scarecrow, giving it a purple hue, and he even licked a white fence, transforming it into a vibrant rainbow.

The farmyard turned into a whimsical wonderland, with colourful objects scattered throughout. The animals delighted in the ever-changing landscape, eagerly awaiting Charlie's next lickin' adventure.

But as the days passed, Charlie began to realize that his constant lickin' had unintended consequences. The colours he applied to the farm were attracting the attention of mischievous city squirrels who saw the vibrant hues as an invitation to play.

These squirrels, known for their pranks, turned the farm into their personal playground. They swung from the rainbow fence, raced through the purple scarecrow's arms, and even rolled in the green wheelbarrow.

The farm animals, while initially entertained, grew weary of the squirrelly shenanigans. They turned to Charlie for help, hoping that his lickin' expertise could save the day.

With a determined look in his eye, Charlie set off on a lickin' mission. He knew that to restore order, he had to outwit the squirrels with his ingenious lickin' skills.

Charlie started with the rainbow fence, giving it a lick that transformed it into a plain wooden structure. The squirrels, confused by the sudden change, hesitated before finding another colourful target.

Next, Charlie turned his attention to the purple scarecrow. He gave it a lick that made it blend in with the fields, leaving the squirrels bewildered as they searched for their beloved playmate.

Finally, Charlie approached the green wheelbarrow. He licked it with precision, returning it to its original yellow hue. The squirrels, disappointed by the sudden lack of excitement, scampered away in search of new adventures.

The farmyard erupted in cheers and applause as Charlie's lickin' skills saved the day. The animals gathered around him, praising his quick thinking and marvelling at his unique talent. His lickin' adventures were celebrated, and he was hailed as the saviour of the farm from the mischievous squirrels.

And so, the farm thrived with laughter and colour, thanks to Charlie's lickin' adventures. Visitors from far and wide would come to witness his extraordinary talent, marvelling at the chicken who had a knack for turning the ordinary into the extraordinary. After all, life is always more exciting when you're lickin' things!

THE DOG WHO WAS STUCK ON A LOG

As Max roamed the riverbank, he noticed a log floating lazily downstream. Eager to investigate, he leaped onto the log, wagging his tail in excitement. But as fate would have it, the log began to drift away from the safety of the riverbank, with Max perched precariously on top.

"Uh-oh," Max yelped, realizing he was now stuck on a log floating on the river. Panic quickly set in, and he began to paddle his paws in a futile attempt to steer the log back to shore. But no matter how hard he paddled, the log seemed determined to take him on an unexpected adventure.

As Max floated along, he couldn't help but notice the interesting sights that unfolded around him. Ducks quacked in amusement, fish jumped out of the water to catch a glimpse of the canine captain, and even a family of turtles sunning themselves on a rock stopped to wave as Max drifted by.

Max's tail wagged nervously as he scanned the riverbank, hoping to catch sight of his owner, Mr. Johnson. Surely, Mr. Johnson would come to his rescue. But to his dismay, Mr. Johnson was nowhere in sight, and Max was left to navigate the river on his own.

As the log meandered downstream, Max's fear slowly turned into curiosity. He realized that, despite the predicament, he had stumbled upon a brand new world—a watery wonderland filled with adventure and laughter.

As the river carried Max further from home, he encountered a peculiar heron named Henry. Perched on a nearby branch, Henry tilted his head and squawked, "Well, well, what do we have here? A dog on a log! It seems you've found yourself in a rather quacky situation, my friend."

Max, his ears drooping with embarrassment, replied, "I didn't mean to end up on this log. I just wanted to explore, but now I'm stuck! Can you help me, Henry?"

Henry chuckled, his long beak bobbing up and down. "Fear not, young pup. I shall guide you through this river's whimsical wonders. Consider me your trusty, heron-ly guide!"

With Henry's guidance, Max embraced his newfound adventure and discovered that the river had a mischievous sense of humour. The log spun in circles, creating a whirlwind of laughter and giggles. Max howled with joy, his tail wagging furiously as he rode the swirling currents.

Along their journey, Max and Henry encountered a lively group of river otters who invited Max to join their water ballet. Max, always up for a playful challenge, clumsily danced and twirled with the otters, much to their amusement. His comical moves and boundless enthusiasm brought smiles to everyone's faces.

As Max continued his river escapades, he encountered a wise old beaver named Benjamin. Perched on a dam, Benjamin stroked his whiskers thoughtfully and said, "Ah, young adventurer, I see you're enjoying the river's mischievous currents. But remember, laughter and curiosity are the true treasures of life."

Inspired by Benjamin's wisdom, Max continued his journey with newfound purpose. He relished in the river's playful pranks, embracing the laughter and joy that filled each moment.

But as the day turned to dusk, Max's joy was tinged with a hint of longing for home. He missed the familiar warmth of Mr. Johnson's hugs, the scent of his cozy dog bed, and the taste of his favourite treats.

Just as Max was about to resign himself to his fate, a soft voice drifted through the evening air. It was Mr. Johnson, calling out for his furry friend. Max's ears perked up, and he barked with joy, his tail wagging furiously.

As the log approached the riverbank, Mr. Johnson stood at the water's edge, his arms outstretched. With a leap of pure excitement, Max jumped off the log, landing safely in his owner's loving embrace.

The river had provided Max with a memorable adventure, but he was relieved to be back in the arms of his best friend. As they walked home, Max's paws splashing in the shallow water, he couldn't help but reflect on the hilarious journey he had experienced.

And as Max curled up in his cozy dog bed that night, his belly full of treats and his heart full of love, he drifted off to sleep with a contented smile.

THE BEE WHO DID A WEE

Benny the Bee did had a terrible habit of weeing everywhere he went. Now, you might be wondering how such a little bee could do such a big wee, but Benny's wee was like a magical waterfall that never seemed to end!

It all started on a day when Benny was out collecting nectar from the beautiful flowers. As he flew from one blossom to another, he felt a strange sensation in his tiny bee bladder. "Oh dear," Benny muttered to himself. "I really need to go for a wee!"

Without thinking much, Benny let it all out, and to his surprise, a huge gush of wee sprayed out like a little fountain. "Wow!" Benny exclaimed, staring at the puddle of wee on the flower. "That's quite impressive!"

Unknown to Benny, a group of busy ladybugs was passing by, and they were not too pleased about their encounter with the unexpected shower. "Eek! A bee with a sprinkler!" cried one ladybug, shaking the wee off her tiny red wings.

Benny felt a bit embarrassed but couldn't help giggling at the sight of the ladybugs trying to dry off. He couldn't resist testing out his newfound wee-power again, and with a twinkle in his bee eyes, he aimed at a nearby leaf. Sure enough, another jet of wee shot out, landing right on the leaf.

"Ha! I bet I can hit that rock over there," Benny said playfully, flying closer to his target. He took careful aim and, with a triumphant cheer, sent a wee-stream soaring through the air, splashing onto the rock.

To Benny's surprise, the other bees in the hive were quite amazed by his special talent. "Benny, you've got quite the aim!" said Buzz, the wise old bee who was the hive leader. "You could be the best wee-shooter of all time."

With a newfound sense of purpose, Benny decided to embrace his special gift. He practiced his wee-shooting skills every day, hitting flower petals, leaves, and even tiny pebbles. The other bees cheered him on, and Benny's confidence grew.

One day, as Benny was out exploring the meadow, he saw a group of butterflies struggling to find water to drink. "Oh no! They must be so thirsty," Benny said with concern.

Without a second thought, Benny flew over to a nearby puddle and let his wee flow gently, creating a tiny water fountain for the butterflies to drink from. The butterflies were overjoyed, and they thanked Benny with a flutter of their colorful wings.

Word spread quickly about Benny's extraordinary talent, and soon he became a local hero. The bees admired him, and even the ladybugs forgave him for their little mishap. "Benny, you truly have a gift!" said Lily, a kind-hearted bee who was Benny's best friend.

Benny's reputation as the wee-shooting bee reached far and wide. Other insects from neighboring meadows came to witness his incredible talent. Benny even started giving "wee shows," where he would demonstrate his impressive wee-shooting skills to a delighted audience.

However, Benny's new fame also attracted some unexpected attention. A mischievous grasshopper named Greg saw an opportunity to make a fortune by exploiting Benny's gift. "With a wee like that, we can create a whole new watering system for the meadow!" Greg said, rubbing his spindly legs together greedily.

Greg convinced Benny that they could make the meadow a better place by using his wee for watering plants. Benny was thrilled by the idea of helping his friends and agreed to give it a try.

The next day, a huge crowd gathered to watch Benny's grand demonstration. Greg had set up a contraption that would channel Benny's wee to water the plants. "Ready, set, go!" Greg called out, and Benny let his wee flow.

But something went terribly wrong! Instead of a gentle stream, Benny's wee gushed out like a mighty river, flooding the entire meadow! The poor flowers, butterflies, and ladybugs were swept away in a wave of bee-wee.

"Oh no! This is not what I had in mind!" Benny cried out in panic. He quickly stopped his wee and tried to apologize to his friends, who were now soggy and wet. "I'm so sorry! I didn't mean for this to happen!" Benny said, feeling terrible for causing such chaos.

Buzz, Lily, and the other bees rushed to Benny's side to comfort him. "It's okay, Benny. We know you didn't mean any harm," Buzz said gently. "But maybe it's best to stick to using your wee for smaller, more fun things." Benny nodded, feeling relieved that his friends forgave him. From that day on, he continued to use his wee for little acts of kindness, like watering thirsty flowers and creating tiny puddles for his insect friends to enjoy.

Whenever someone asked about his wee-shooting skills, Benny would chuckle and say, "Well, I did a wee once that caused quite a splash, but now I use it for much smaller and happier things. After all, it's the little acts of kindness that make the biggest difference in the world!

THE FROG WHO GOT LOST IN THE FOG

Freddy was known for jumping, he was a Frog after all, but he also was an explorer! Little did he know that one day, his curiosity would lead him to a truly ribbit-ing adventure—a journey inside the belly of a gigantic frog!

It all began on a sunny morning when Freddy hopped from lily pad to lily pad, exploring the nooks and crannies of his watery home. As he leaped through the air, he spotted a large frog with bulging eyes and a wide grin sitting near the edge of the pond.

Freddy's eyes widened with excitement. He had never seen a frog as big as this one before. He just had to take a closer look! Without hesitation, he hopped toward the giant frog, eager to inspect every wrinkle and bump on its skin.

But as Freddy reached the massive creature, he found himself suddenly sucked into the frog's gaping mouth. He gasped for air, his heart racing, realizing that he had been swallowed whole! Freddy was now trapped inside the belly of the big frog.

Inside the frog's belly, Freddy squirmed and wriggled, trying to find a way out. But no matter how much he hopped and jumped, the slippery walls of the frog's stomach kept him trapped.

Freddy's eyes darted around the belly, and to his surprise, he found himself surrounded by a whole community of lost items—glasses, socks, and even a tiny umbrella. It seemed that the big frog had a habit of swallowing everything in its path!

As Freddy explored further, he stumbled upon a group of chatty worms who had also found themselves trapped inside the belly. The worms welcomed Freddy with open arms—or rather, open segments—and together they formed an unlikely alliance.

"We must find a way out of here!" exclaimed Wormy, the self-proclaimed leader of the group. "We'll wriggle, squirm, and wiggle our way to freedom!"

And so, Freddy and the worms embarked on their daring escape plan. They used their combined strength and determination to push against the slimy walls of the belly, hoping to create enough pressure to force the big frog to cough them out.

As they pushed and wriggled, the frog's belly rumbled with discontent. It let out a series of enormous burps that echoed through the pond, catching the attention of the other frogs nearby.

Curious about the unusual sounds, a group of frogs gathered around the big frog, their eyes wide with astonishment. They watched in awe as the big frog burped repeatedly, propelling Freddy and the worms out of its belly one by one.

With a final burp, Freddy soared through the air, landing safely on a lily pad. He turned to the worms, who were also happily reunited with the earth, and they exchanged victorious high-fives—or high-segments in the worms' case.

As the crowd of frogs cheered and applauded, Freddy couldn't help but feel a sense of relief. He had managed to escape the belly of the big frog with the help of his newfound worm friends.

Freddy, now a local celebrity, embraced his newfound fame with a lighthearted spirit. He entertained the other frogs with his comical jumps and daring antics, always ready to bring laughter to the pond.

As the sun set over the lily pad-filled pond, casting a warm golden glow, Freddy hopped onto a lily pad, surrounded by his adoring frog friends. He knew that life was full of surprises and adventures, and no matter what ribbit-ing situation he found himself in, he would always find a way to laugh and leap forward.

THE WHALE WHO LEARNT HOW TO SAIL

In the vast and shimmering ocean, there lived a rather unusual whale named Walter. Now, Walter was not your ordinary whale. While other whales swam gracefully through the water, Walter dreamed of sailing the high seas like a swashbuckling pirate. Little did he know that his quest to become a sailing whale would lead to a hilarious adventure that would have everyone in the ocean giggling with glee.

You see, Walter spent his days observing the boats sailing above him. He marvelled at their billowing sails and the way they glided through the waves. Deep down, he yearned to join them, to experience the thrill of sailing firsthand.

As Walter bobbed near the surface, he spotted a group of dolphins playfully leaping through the air. Inspiration struck him like a bolt of lightning. If dolphins could leap, why couldn't a whale sail?

Determined to fulfil his seafaring dreams, Walter set off on a mission to become the first sailing whale. With a flick of his mighty tail, he propelled himself towards the nearest beach, ready to learn the art of sailing from the humans.

As Walter arrived at the beach, he couldn't help but notice a group of children learning to sail small boats. Their laughter and shouts of excitement filled the air, and Walter knew he had come to the right place.

With a mischievous glint in his eye, Walter approached the

children, causing them to gasp in surprise. "Hello there, young sailors! I'm Walter, the whale who wants to sail. Can you teach me?"

The children burst into laughter, hardly believing their eyes. A talking whale? This was going to be the adventure of a lifetime! They eagerly agreed to help Walter learn how to sail.

The children explained the basics of sailing—the wind, the sails, and how to manoeuvre the boat. Walter listened intently, his tail swishing with excitement.

Now, the children had a brilliant idea. They decided to construct a special sail just for Walter. With their creative minds at work, they fashioned a sail out of a colourful beach towel and secured it to Walter's dorsal fin. Walter beamed with joy, ready to set sail on his grand adventure.

With the children by his side, Walter dipped back into the ocean, his makeshift sail catching the wind. The children clung to his side, feeling the exhilaration of the wind whipping through their hair as Walter propelled them forward.

As they sailed across the sparkling waves, Walter couldn't contain his laughter. He felt like the king of the sea, gliding through the water with the grace of a seafaring captain. The other sea creatures watched in awe as Walter, the sailing whale, passed by.

But as the sun began to set, a curious sight caught Walter's eye—a pod of dolphins gracefully leaping in the distance. Inspired by their acrobatics, Walter decided to try something daring—whale-leaps!

With a mighty thrust, Walter launched himself out of the water, his sail billowing in the wind. The children squealed with delight as they soared through the air, higher and higher. They were now sailing through the sky!

Their laughter echoed across the ocean, reaching the ears of all the sea creatures. Dolphins, turtles, and even seagulls flocked to witness this spectacle. The sky was filled with joyous cheers and the resounding sound of Walter's leaping antics.

But as the excitement reached its peak, a sudden gust of wind caught Walter off guard. His sail became tangled, and he lost control of his leap. With a mighty splash, Walter crashed back into the ocean, causing a colossal wave to wash over the beach.

The children clung to Walter, soaked but unharmed, and burst into laughter. Walter, now fully immersed in the water, giggled along with them. It seemed his sailing adventure had taken an unexpected turn, but it was a joyful turn nonetheless.

As they regrouped, a wise old turtle named Terry swam by. With a twinkle in his eye, he said, "Ah, young Walter, I see you've discovered the joy of sailing, even if it does involve a few belly-flops. Remember, laughter and the spirit of adventure are what make life truly remarkable."

Walter nodded, his heart brimming with gratitude for Terry's wise words. He realized that even though he hadn't mastered the art of sailing, the joy and laughter he experienced on his journey were worth more than any seafaring skill.

Walter continued his sailing adventures, often accompanied by a flock of seagulls and a pod of dolphins who had been inspired by his antics. The sea creatures eagerly awaited his sail-filled leaps, eager to witness the spectacle and join in the laughter.

THE FOX WHO WORE FLUFFY SOCKS

Feliz adored wearing fluffy socks! Yes, you heard it right—fluffy socks! And little did he know that his obsession with cozy footwear would lead to a hilarious adventure that would have everyone in the forest giggling with delight.

One day as Felix strutted through the forest, his fluffy socks bouncing with every step, he couldn't help but notice the peculiar stares from the other animals. They gazed at him, their eyes wide with surprise and confusion.

"What's wrong with wearing fluffy socks?" Felix muttered to himself, adjusting his mismatched pair with pride.

But little did he know that his fluffy socks would soon cause quite a commotion. You see, word of Felix's fashion statement spread throughout the forest like wildfire, and the other animals grew curious about this fluffy sock trend.

One by one, the forest dwellers approached Felix, each wanting to try on a pair of fluffy socks for themselves. The squirrels, the rabbits, even the wise old owl—they all wanted a taste of the fluffy sock frenzy!

Felix, feeling a sense of responsibility as the fluffy sock fashion pioneer, agreed to organize a Fluffy Sock Fashion Show in the heart of the forest. The animals buzzed with excitement, donning their most fashionable outfits and eagerly awaiting their turn on the leafy runway.

As the fashion show commenced, the forest creatures paraded in their fluffy socks, striking poses and showing off their unique styles. The squirrels wore bright blue socks with acorn patterns, the rabbits sported pink socks adorned with carrot designs, and the wise old owl waddled gracefully in her fluffy gray socks.

The forest erupted in laughter and applause as each animal showcased their wackiest and most creative socks. The fashion show became a riotous celebration of individuality and, of course, fabulous footwear.

But amidst the laughter and merriment, a sneaky raccoon named Ricky had a devious plan brewing in his mind. Ricky, known for his mischievous ways, couldn't resist the allure of the fluffy socks. He wanted them all for himself!

Under the cover of darkness, Ricky snuck into Felix's fluffy sock collection. With a gleeful grin, he stole every single pair, leaving Felix and the other animals sockless and bewildered.

The next morning, as the animals awoke to find their fluffy socks missing, a wave of panic swept through the forest. The Fluffy Sock Fashion Show was just days away, and without the iconic socks, the event seemed doomed.

Felix, determined not to let Ricky's antics ruin the show, called an emergency meeting with the forest animals. They brainstormed and hatched a plan to retrieve the stolen socks and save the fashion show.

With Felix as their fearless leader, the animals set out on a hilarious adventure to track down Ricky and reclaim their beloved fluffy socks.

Through thick forests, across babbling brooks, and over mossy rocks, the animals followed Ricky's trail, leaving no stone unturned. They encountered comedic mishaps along the way—a squirrel tripped on his own fluffy tail, a rabbit got tangled in a thicket of thorns, and poor Felix even stepped on a banana peel and tumbled headfirst into a muddy puddle. But nothing could dampen their determination.

Finally, they reached Ricky's secret hideout—an old tree stump hidden deep within the forest. With the element of surprise on their side, they devised a cunning plan to distract Ricky and retrieve the fluffy socks.

Felix, always the quick thinker, came up with a genius idea. He whispered a plan to the wise old owl, who hooted in agreement. The owl swooped down, pretending to be an injured bird, while the rest of the animals stealthily crept into the hideout.

As Ricky rushed to aid the "injured" owl, the animals pounced into action. With a flurry of tails and paws, they grabbed the stolen socks and made a swift exit, leaving Ricky dumbfounded and sockless.

Back at the heart of the forest, the animals celebrated their victory. They adorned their paws and hooves with their reclaimed fluffy socks, giggling and prancing around in delight. The Fluffy Sock Fashion Show was back on!

On the day of the show, the forest creatures gathered once again, their fluffy socks now even more special, as they represented resilience and unity. The runway came alive with vibrant colours and hilarious sock-themed outfits.

Felix, beaming with pride, stood at the center of the fashion show, his fluffy socks more fabulous than ever. The laughter and applause echoed through the trees, filling the forest with joy.

And as night fell and the forest creatures settled into their cozy dens, Felix curled up, his paws snug in his fluffy socks, feeling a deep sense of contentment. He knew that he had brought laughter, fashion, and a whole lot of silliness to the forest, and that his love for fluffy socks would forever be remembered as a tale of unity, resilience, and fabulous fashion in the hearts of the forest animals.

THE MOUSE IN THE HAUNTED HOUSE

While other mice scurried away from danger, Marvin had an adventurous spirit that often landed him in hilarious situations. One dark and stormy night, as the wind howled and the lightning cracked across the sky, Marvin found himself standing in front of the haunted house. Its windows were boarded up, and the ivy crawled up the walls like twisted fingers. The local mice had always whispered tales of ghosts, ghouls, and other spooky creatures that roamed the halls of the haunted house.

But Marvin, being the brave and curious little mouse that he was, couldn't resist the allure of the mysterious dwelling. With a flick of his whiskers and a determined squeak, he scurried through the front door, ready to uncover the secrets hidden within.

As Marvin ventured deeper into the house, the creaking floorboards echoed with his tiny footsteps. The air was heavy with an eerie silence, broken only by the occasional hoot of an owl outside. Every shadow seemed to hold a hidden surprise, and Marvin's heart raced with both fear and excitement.

Suddenly, a gust of wind rattled the windows, causing a cobweb to brush against Marvin's face. Startled, he let out a yelp and leaped onto a dusty bookshelf, sending a cascade of books tumbling to the floor. The commotion stirred up a cloud of dust, creating a mini whirlwind that made Marvin sneeze.

"Achoo!" sneezed Marvin, his tiny sneeze echoing through the empty halls. Little did he know that his sneeze had awakened the mischievous spirits that dwelled within the haunted house.

With a flicker of light, the ghosts materialized before Marvin. But instead of the terrifying creatures he had imagined, he was met with a group of friendly and playful apparitions.

"Hello there, little mouse!" one ghost said, its voice echoing with a friendly tone. "We're the ghosts of this haunted house, and we've been waiting for someone like you to join our spooky party!"

Marvin blinked his tiny eyes in surprise. "You... you're not scary ghosts?"

The ghosts giggled, their transparent forms swirling in the air. "Oh, we're only scary when we want to be. But right now, we just want to have some fun!"

And fun they had indeed! The ghosts showed Marvin their secret hideouts, which were filled with tricks, pranks, and all sorts of ghostly delights. Marvin laughed as the ghosts played tricks on each other, turning invisible objects visible and making objects float through the air.

But the real fun began when the ghosts challenged Marvin to a game of hide-and-seek. With their ethereal forms, they disappeared and reappeared in the most unexpected places, causing Marvin to chase them through the house in fits of laughter.

As the night wore on, Marvin's fear melted away, replaced by a deep sense of camaraderie with his new ghostly friends. They taught him how to float through walls, leaving tiny mouse-shaped imprints in their wake. Marvin couldn't believe he was having the time of his life in a haunted house!

But just as the moon reached its peak in the sky, a distant bell tolled, signalling the arrival of dawn. The ghosts' faces grew sombre as they realized their time together was coming to an end.

"We must return to our resting place," said the ghostly leader, a shimmering figure with a mischievous grin. "But we'll always remember the brave little mouse who brought laughter to our haunted house."

Marvin nodded, his whiskers twitching with a mix of sadness and joy. He knew that his adventure had come to an end, but the memories would stay with him forever.

As Marvin bid farewell to his ghostly friends, he scurried out of the haunted house, back into the safety of the forest. The sun began to rise, casting a warm glow on the trees and banishing the darkness that had enveloped the haunted house.

And as the nights grew longer and the winds whispered stories of the haunted house, Marvin's story continued to be passed down from generation to generation. Each time it was told, the forest creatures erupted in laughter, cherishing the memory of the brave little mouse who found friendship and laughter in the most unexpected place.

And as for Marvin, he lived out his days in the forest, regaling his fellow mice with stories of his ghostly adventures. He had learned that sometimes, the scariest places held the most delightful surprises, and the most unexpected friendships could be formed in the unlikeliest of settings.

So, the next time you pass by a haunted house, remember the tale of Marvin the mouse and his hilarious journey. For who knows, maybe you'll find laughter and friendship where you least expect it!

THE BUNNY WHO LOVED HONEY

Benny had a particular weakness — he had an insatiable appetite for honey. Not just a fondness, mind you, but an all-consuming, borderline-obsessive love for the sticky golden goodness. And so, it was no surprise that Benny's life took a hilarious turn when he stumbled upon an endless supply of honey.

One sunny morning, as Benny hopped through the meadow, his twitching nose caught a whiff of something irresistible. He followed the mouthwatering scent, and to his sheer delight, he discovered a hidden beehive tucked away under a flowering bush. The beehive was overflowing with honey, its golden streams practically calling out his name.

Without thinking twice, Benny dove headfirst into the beehive, his eyes shining with anticipation. He devoured spoonful after spoonful of honey, his little paws covered in sticky goodness. The honey was so deliciously sweet that Benny couldn't stop himself. He ate and ate, oblivious to the consequences of his honey-fuelled binge.

As Benny continued his honey feast, the bees, who were not too thrilled about the bunny's honey theft, began to swarm around him. They buzzed angrily, their tiny wings creating a furious symphony in the meadow. Benny, lost in his honey-induced euphoria, failed to notice the growing cloud of bees surrounding him.

Suddenly, one brave bee, let's call her Bella, decided to take matters into her own wings. She flew right up to Benny's twitching nose and stung him with a sharp little sting. Benny let out a startled yelp and jumped back, his eyes watering from the sting. But his love for honey outweighed the temporary discomfort, and he went back to his honey feast, ignoring the warning signs.

Undeterred by Bella's sting, Benny continued to gorge himself on honey, completely oblivious to the growing swarm of bees. The bees, now in full attack mode, launched a coordinated aerial assault on the honey-obsessed bunny. They buzzed around him, dive-bombing and zigzagging, trying to protect their precious honey.

But Benny, lost in a sticky honey haze, thought the bees were playing an elaborate game of tag. He giggled with delight as they zoomed past him, completely oblivious to the danger he was in.

Meanwhile, the other animals in the meadow had gathered to watch the spectacle unfolding. They watched with a mixture of amusement and disbelief as Benny hopped around, covered in honey, and chased by a furious swarm of bees. Squirrels dropped their acorns in fits of laughter, while birds tweeted about the bunny who had bitten off more honey than he could chew.

Amidst the chaos, a wise old owl named Oliver perched on a branch, observing the commotion with a twinkle in his eyes. He hooted, "Benny, my dear friend, sometimes love can lead us down a sticky path."

Finally, after what seemed like an eternity of honey-driven madness, Benny's belly couldn't handle another spoonful. He plopped down on the grass, his belly bulging with honey. The bees, satisfied that their honey was safe once again, flew back to their hive, leaving Benny in a sticky, sugary mess.

Benny, now sticky from head to toe, looked around at the animals staring at him, their laughter echoing through the meadow. With a sheepish grin, he admitted, "I guess I bit off more honey than I could chew."

The meadow erupted in laughter, the animals rolling on the ground, tears streaming down their faces. Benny, now humbled by his honey-filled misadventure, joined in the laughter, his sticky paws flailing in the air.

From that day on, Benny learned to appreciate honey in moderation, and the animals in the meadow would chuckle and shake their heads whenever they spotted a glimmer of honey in his eyes. And as for Bella the bee, well, she became Benny's trusted friend, teaching him that sometimes, a little sting of reality is needed to save us from ourselves.

THE FISH WHO HAD A WISH

Now, Finn was not your ordinary fish. While other fish swam gracefully, Finn had a wild imagination and a mischievous streak that often landed him in hilarious situations. And little did he know that his latest adventure—a fish with an extraordinary wish —would lead to a tale of laughter and underwater escapades.

Finn was an adventurous fish who loved exploring every nook and cranny of the coral reef. One sunny day, as he darted through the colourful coral, he noticed an old, wise turtle named Terry resting on a rock. Curiosity piqued, Finn swam closer.

"Hello, wise Terry! I have a wish, and I'm sure you can help me," exclaimed Finn, his fins wiggling with excitement.

Terry chuckled, his wise eyes twinkling. "Well, young Finn, tell me your wish, and I shall see what I can do."

Finn took a deep breath and declared, "I want to fly!"

Terry's wrinkled face broke into a grin. "Fly? My dear Finn, fish are meant to swim, not fly. But if you're determined, I may have a solution."

With a knowing smile, Terry explained that there was a legendary fish who possessed the power to grant extraordinary wishes. The fabled fish, known as Wilbur the Wise, resided in a hidden cave at the deepest part of the ocean.

Eager to have his wish granted, Finn bid farewell to Terry and embarked on a daring quest to find Wilbur the Wise. He swam through coral forests, glided over seagrass meadows, and braved the depths of the mysterious ocean.

After an exhilarating journey filled with encounters with mischievous seahorses and playful dolphins, Finn reached the entrance of the hidden cave. With a deep breath, he entered the dark abyss, where he found Wilbur the Wise—a large, majestic fish with a long, flowing beard.

Wilbur looked at Finn with wise eyes and asked, "Why have you come, young fish?"

Finn, bubbling with excitement, blurted out, "I want to fly! Can you grant my wish, oh Wise One?"

Wilbur chuckled, his voice resonating through the cave. "Fly, you say? Fish are not meant to soar through the skies. But I have an alternative that might satisfy your wish."

With a wave of his fin, Wilbur summoned a magical pearl from the depths of the cave. The pearl shimmered with an enchanting glow as it floated towards Finn.

"Swallow this pearl, young Finn, and you shall discover a new way to experience the world," Wilbur said with a cryptic smile.

Curiosity outweighed caution, and Finn gulped down the magical pearl. Suddenly, a tingling sensation coursed through his scales, and his fins began to flutter like wings. To his surprise, Finn found himself floating effortlessly above the ocean's surface.

Finn's eyes widened with wonder as he soared through the sky, feeling the wind ruffling his scales. He looped and twirled, giggling with delight, as the birds above watched in amazement.

But as Finn revelled in his newfound ability, a mischievous seagull named Sammy spotted him from afar. Sammy, always seeking attention, decided to join Finn in the aerial escapades. With a raucous squawk, he swooped down and startled poor Finn, causing him to lose control and spiral into a nose-dive.

Finn plummeted into the water with a splash, his wings fizzling into fins once more. He looked up, dishevelled and dripping wet, as Sammy cackled from above.

Undeterred by the mishap, Finn swam back to the surface, his fins determined. He realized that flying might not be his true calling, but swimming with his fellow fish in the ocean's depths brought him immense joy.

Finn returned to Terry, the wise turtle, and recounted his adventure, emphasizing the hilarity of his failed flight. Terry laughed heartily, his shell shaking with amusement.

"You see, Finn," Terry said, "sometimes our wishes lead us on unexpected journeys, and the lessons we learn along the way are far more valuable than the wish itself."

Finn nodded, a smile spreading across his face. He understood that it wasn't the ability to fly that mattered but the laughter, joy, and lessons he gained throughout his daring quest.

From that day forward, Finn embraced his fishy nature with a renewed sense of excitement. He swam through the coral reefs, performing comical somersaults and entertaining his fellow fish with his adventurous tales. And whenever he spotted a mischievous seagull in the distance, Finn couldn't help but chuckle, knowing that his wish to fly had led him to the most unexpected and humorous encounters. Life is meant to be a splashing good time!

THE BABOON WHO FLEW AWAY ON A BALLOON

While his friends swung from tree to tree, Benny dreamed of soaring through the sky like a graceful bird. Little did he know that his peculiar wish—a baboon flying away on a balloon—would lead to an uproarious adventure that would have everyone in the jungle laughing with joy.

It all began when Benny stumbled upon a patch of vibrant, colourful balloons that had drifted into the jungle. His eyes lit up with excitement as he gazed at the balloons bobbing in the gentle breeze. Inspiration struck him like a coconut falling from a tree.

"I'm going to fly!" Benny exclaimed, his tail wagging with excitement. He scrambled to gather the balloons and began to tie them together, creating his own makeshift hot air balloon.

His jungle friends, a group of curious monkeys, gathered around him, their eyes wide with astonishment. "Benny, are you sure about this?" asked Marvin, the wise old monkey.

Benny beamed with confidence. "Of course! I've always wanted to fly, and today is the day!"

And so, with a mischievous grin and a balloon-filled contraption, Benny embarked on his hilarious quest to take flight. The monkeys watched in both awe and concern as Benny hopped into the balloon's basket, ready to fulfil his dream.

With a final tug on the ropes, Benny let go of the jungle floor and slowly ascended into the sky. The monkeys waved below, their faces filled with a mix of amazement and worry.

As Benny floated higher and higher, he couldn't contain his excitement. The wind whistled through his fur, and his laughter echoed through the jungle. "I'm flying! Look at me!"

But as Benny marvelled at his newfound aerial adventure, he failed to notice that a mischievous toucan named Tilly had decided to join him. With a swoop and a squawk, Tilly landed in the balloon basket, causing Benny to jolt with surprise.

"What are you doing here, Tilly?" Benny asked, his eyes wide.

Tilly, known for her love of chaos and adventure, cackled mischievously. "Well, Benny, flying looks like too much fun to miss! Besides, who can resist the chance to cause a bit of feathered mayhem?"

Benny chuckled, realizing that he had a partner in crime for his airborne escapades. With Tilly by his side, the two set off on a series of wild and comical adventures high above the jungle canopy.

They soared through fluffy white clouds, chasing their shadows and playfully tossing mangoes at unsuspecting animals below. Benny and Tilly performed acrobatic stunts, flipping and twirling in the sky, much to the amazement of the jungle creatures.

But their laughter-filled journey took an unexpected turn when they flew too close to a tall, thorny tree. With a loud pop, one of the balloons burst, causing the balloon basket to tilt precariously to one side.

Benny and Tilly clung onto the basket, their eyes wide with panic. The balloon wobbled and swayed, threatening to send them crashing to the ground. They glanced at each other, their faces pale with fear.

Just as they thought their adventure had taken a prickly turn, a group of helpful monkeys swung to the rescue. With their nimble tails and quick thinking, they managed to steady the balloon basket and bring Benny and Tilly safely back to the jungle floor.

The monkeys erupted in laughter, their playful chatters filling the air. Benny and Tilly joined in, relieved and grateful for their heroic rescue.

THE BEAVER WHO HAD A FEVER

While his fellow beavers diligently built dams and gathered food, Benny was known for his knack for getting into silly and hilarious situations. Little did he know that his latest adventure—a beaver with a fever—would lead to a laugh-out-loud tale that would have everyone in the forest chuckling with delight.

One morning, as Benny eagerly joined his beaver friends in their daily activities, he noticed a strange sensation—a tickle in his snout, a rumble in his tummy, and an itchy feeling all over. Confused by these strange symptoms, Benny scratched his furry head, wondering what could be the cause.

Unbeknownst to Benny, he had come down with a case of Beaver Fever—a rare condition that caused uncontrollable laughter and a series of comical mishaps.

As Benny's fever escalated, his normally calm and collected demeanour transformed into a frenzy of uncontrollable giggles. He wobbled around, bumping into trees and splashing into the river with hilarious splutters.

The other beavers watched in both amusement and bewilderment as Benny's fever-induced antics grew wilder by the minute. They gathered around, trying to make sense of the situation.

"Hey, Benny! What's going on?" asked Bobby, a fellow beaver, struggling to hold back his laughter.

Benny, snickering uncontrollably, tried to explain his predicament between bursts of giggles. "I've got Beaver Fever! It's like an itch that tickles and makes you laugh...a lot!"

The beavers burst into laughter, their tails slapping the water with glee. They had never seen Benny like this before, and the forest echoed with their joyous chortles.

As Benny's laughter echoed through the trees, word of his Beaver Fever spread throughout the forest. Animals from all walks of life flocked to witness the hilarity unfold. Squirrels chattered with glee, birds swooped and chirped, and even the wise old owl couldn't help but hoot in amusement.

Embracing the unexpected turn of events, the forest animals organized a grand "Fever Fiesta" to celebrate Benny's contagious laughter. They decorated the trees with strings of acorns and arranged a banquet of berries, nuts, and tasty treats.

As Benny arrived at the Fever Fiesta, he couldn't help but chuckle at the sight before him. The forest glowed with laughter and excitement. Animals danced and twirled, their laughter filling the air as they joined Benny in his infectious fever-induced merriment.

There were squirrel acrobats tumbling from branch to branch, birds conducting a symphony of hoots and chirps, and even a family of rabbits hopping in rhythm to the laughter-filled beat.

But as the festivities reached their peak, Benny's laughter took an unexpected turn. With each giggle, tiny bubbles emerged from his mouth, floating through the air like shimmering orbs of joy.

The animals stared in amazement, their laughter momentarily silenced by the spectacle before them. The forest transformed into a mesmerizing bubble-filled wonderland.

Benny, his eyes twinkling with mischief, couldn't resist the temptation. With a big gulp of air, he blew a gust of laughter-induced bubbles towards the gathered animals. The forest erupted in a sea of giggles and bubbles, as the creatures batted the iridescent orbs and chased them through the trees.

As the bubbles floated lazily through the air, Benny couldn't help but laugh even harder. He twirled and spun, creating bubble tornadoes that had the animals in stitches.

But as the sun began to set, casting a warm golden glow upon the forest, Benny's laughter began to subside. His Beaver Fever was fading, leaving behind fond memories and aching sides.

As the animals bid Benny farewell, they thanked him for the unforgettable laughter-filled adventure. Benny beamed with pride, knowing that his Beaver Fever had brought joy and merriment to the entire forest.

And as he curled up in his cozy beaver lodge, Benny reflected on the day's events. The next time you find yourself in fits of laughter, remember the tale of Benny the Beaver and his unforgettable Beaver Fever. Embrace the laughter, share it with friends, and let your giggles fill the world with joy. After all, life is meant to be a hilarious adventure!

THE SHARK WHO COULD BARK

As other sharks glided through the water silently, Sherman had a peculiar talent—he could bark! Yes, you heard it right—a barking shark! Little did he know that his unusual ability would lead to a comical and uproarious adventure that would have everyone in the underwater kingdom laughing their scales off.

Sherman swam through the ocean with his sharp teeth and sleek gray body, but every time he tried to say "hello" to his fishy friends, all that came out was a series of funny barks. His fish friends would swim away in confusion, leaving poor Sherman feeling misunderstood and, well, a little lonely.

One sunny day, as Sherman barked his way through a school of colourful fish, he spotted a wise old octopus named Oliver. Known for his knowledge of underwater wonders, Oliver was the perfect companion to help Sherman understand his barking conundrum.

"Oliver, my friend!" Sherman called out with a series of excited barks. "I need your help! Why can't I speak fish like everyone else?"

Oliver's eyes twinkled as he watched Sherman's funny attempts at communication. "Sherman, my dear shark, it seems you have a unique gift—a talent for barking!"

Sherman's eyes widened in surprise. "But I want to speak fish, not bark like a dog!"

Oliver chuckled, his tentacles swirling in amusement. "Ah, but imagine the possibilities, Sherman! With your barking talent, you can communicate with creatures from all corners of the ocean. You're not just a shark, you're a barking sensation!"

Inspired by Oliver's wise words, Sherman decided to embrace his barking gift and set off on a hilarious journey through the underwater kingdom. He travelled from the vibrant coral reefs to the mysterious depths, encountering all sorts of comical characters along the way.

First, Sherman met a crab named Clive, who loved to tap dance on the sandy ocean floor. Clive was delighted by Sherman's barks and taught him some fancy dance moves in return. Together, they formed an underwater dance troupe, wowing the ocean creatures with their synchronized barks and tap-dancing routines.

Next, Sherman swam across an energetic seahorse named Sally, who had dreams of becoming an underwater rockstar. Sally's eyes sparkled when she heard Sherman's barks and realized they could form the basis of an extraordinary musical collaboration. With Sherman's barks as the beat and Sally's melodic tunes, they formed the first-ever underwater bark-and-roll band. They rocked the ocean floor with their hilarious performances, and fish from miles away flocked to hear their unique sound.

As Sherman's fame spread throughout the underwater kingdom, he found himself invited to all sorts of peculiar events. He attended an underwater comedy festival, where he barked out punchlines that had the clownfish rolling with laughter. He even participated in a synchronized swimming competition, using his barks as the rhythm for a mesmerizing underwater routine that earned him a perfect score.

But as Sherman barked his way through endless adventures, he began to long for something more meaningful. He realized that while his barking talent brought joy and laughter, he wanted to use it to make a difference in the ocean.

One day, as Sherman swam past a group of sad dolphins, he knew he had found his calling. With his infectious barks, he brought smiles to their faces, and the underwater kingdom echoed with laughter once again. Inspired by the dolphins' happiness, Sherman joined forces with them to spread joy and laughter to all the creatures of the sea.

Together, they organized a grand underwater carnival—an event filled with games, music, and, of course, Sherman's famous barking performances. The ocean creatures swam from far and wide to be a part of the laughter-filled celebration.

As the carnival came to an end, Sherman realized that he had fulfilled his purpose. He had brought laughter and happiness to the underwater kingdom, and his barking talent had made a true difference in the lives of his fishy friends.

Sherman continued to explore the depths of the ocean, spreading joy with his barks. He taught other sharks to bark, formed underwater choirs, and even became a motivational speaker, encouraging creatures big and small to embrace their unique talents and find their own funny voices. So, the next time you find yourself underwater, listen closely for the sound of laughter and barking—it might just be Sherman the barking shark, spreading joy and turning the ocean into a sea of smiles.

THE SWAN WHO MOWED THE LAWN

Sylvia the swan had an unusual obsession—she loved mowing the lawn! Little did she know that her unusual hobby—a swan who mowed the lawn—would lead to a hilarious adventure that would have everyone in the animal kingdom quacking with laughter.

Every morning, while the other swans preened their feathers and basked in the sun, Sylvia would waddle onto the shore, don a tiny lawnmower helmet, and start her trusty lawnmower. With a determined expression on her face, she would march across the grass, meticulously mowing every blade, as if she were a professional gardener in disguise.

The other animals of the pond couldn't believe their eyes. Ducks would quack in confusion, turtles would blink in disbelief, and even the wise old owl hooted in amusement.

"What's she doing? Is she lost?" wondered Sammy, a curious turtle who watched Sylvia from his cozy spot on a nearby log.

The pond's inhabitants couldn't resist investigating Sylvia's peculiar behaviour. One by one, they gathered around the lawn as she meticulously maneuvered her lawnmower, expertly avoiding blades of grass.

"Excuse me, Sylvia," quacked a curious duck named Daisy. "What on earth are you doing? Swans don't mow lawns!"

Sylvia paused, her feathers fluffed with pride. "Oh, my dear friends, I have discovered the joy of a well-manicured lawn! I find it incredibly satisfying. Plus, it gives me a break from all that swimming."

The animals exchanged bewildered glances, but their confusion quickly turned into laughter. Soon, the entire pond echoed with their amusement.

Embracing the laughter and the curious stares, Sylvia continued her daily routine, mowing the lawn with unwavering determination. The other animals nicknamed her "Sylvia the Lawnmower Swan" and would gather every morning to witness her hilarious attempts.

One fateful day, as Sylvia mowed the lawn with her usual precision, she noticed a peculiar sight—a family of rabbits hopping towards her with a mischievous glint in their eyes.

"Hop aboard, Sylvia! We've got a surprise for you!" giggled Flopsy, the mischievous ringleader of the rabbit family.

Intrigued and always up for an adventure, Sylvia turned off her lawnmower and hopped onto the back of the rabbit's fluffy tail, being whisked away across the meadows.

With Sylvia perched on Flopsy's back, the rabbits led her to a neighbouring garden. And what a sight awaited her! The garden was a jungle of overgrown bushes and tangled flowers, desperately in need of her expert lawnmowing skills.

Without hesitation, Sylvia leaped from Flopsy's back and fired up her trusty lawnmower. The blades whirred to life, and Sylvia got to work, transforming the unkempt garden into a perfectly manicured paradise.

As Sylvia mowed, the garden's owner—a surprised and slightly bewildered human—watched from a distance, unable to believe his eyes. He couldn't help but burst into laughter at the sight of a swan mowing his lawn.

Word of Sylvia's extraordinary lawnmowing skills spread

throughout the animal kingdom. Soon, animals from far and wide flocked to Sylvia's lawn-mowing performances, eager to witness the hilarity of a swan on a mission.

Animals formed long lines, each awaiting their turn to have Sylvia turn their unkempt gardens into works of art. From hedgehogs with messy hedges to squirrels with overgrown trees, Sylvia's lawnmower buzzed through the animal kingdom, leaving laughter and perfectly trimmed lawns in its wake.

But the most memorable moment came when Sylvia received a special request from the king of the forest—a regal lion named Leo. Leo's majestic mane had grown unruly, and he needed Sylvia's expertise to give him a trim fit for royalty.

With a twinkle in her eye and her lawnmower at the ready, Sylvia fearlessly approached the mighty lion. Leo stood still, his nerves tingling with anticipation as the lawnmower buzzed closer to his magnificent mane.

With the precision of a seasoned barber, Sylvia guided the lawnmower through Leo's mane, trimming it to perfection. The animals gasped in astonishment as the proud lion strutted with newfound confidence, showing off his impeccably styled mane.

MAX THE MULE

"I want to go to school too!" Max exclaimed, his ears perked up with excitement.

With a twinkle in his eye and a mischievous grin, Max trotted over to the car. With his hooves expertly manoeuvring the pedals, he hopped into the driver's seat and turned the ignition key. To his delight, the engine roared to life, and Max found himself behind the wheel of a roaring automobile.

The people near him watched in astonishment as Max, the mule, revved the engine and drove down the street, honking the horn with glee. Children dropped their school bags, parents dropped their coffee mugs, and the entire town erupted into laughter and applause.

As Max approached the school, the children burst out of the building, their eyes wide with astonishment. They couldn't believe their eyes—a mule driving a car! Max parked the car with a triumphant neigh, and the children gathered around in awe.

The school's principal, Mr. Thompson, stepped out, his mustache quivering in disbelief. "Max! What are you doing here? Mules don't go to school!"

Max grinned, his teeth glinting mischievously. "But Mr. Thompson, I want to learn too! I promise to be the best student you've ever seen."

Mr. Thompson couldn't help but chuckle at Max's determination. "Well, Max, if you want to learn, I suppose we can make an exception."

And so, with a wave of his hoof and a twirl of his tail, Max became the first-ever mule enrolled in the town's school. He attended classes alongside the children, his ears perked up with enthusiasm as he soaked up knowledge like a sponge.

In math class, Max's hooves clacked against the floor as he solved equations, often coming up with hilariously unique answers. In science class, he donned a lab coat and goggles, causing the beakers to tremble with excitement as he conducted funny experiments. And in art class, Max's hooves danced across the canvas, creating abstract masterpieces that left the art teacher speechless.

But it wasn't just Max's academic prowess that brought laughter to the school—it was his unique perspective and sense of humour. During recess, Max would entertain his classmates with hilarious tricks, like balancing apples on his nose or performing a one-mule show of "The Three Little Pigs."

The children couldn't get enough of Max's antics, and soon he became the most popular student in school. They would eagerly gather around him during lunch breaks, sharing jokes and stories, their laughter filling the hallways.

But as the school year progressed, Max realized that he wasn't just there to make the children laugh—he wanted to make a difference. He noticed that some of his classmates struggled with their studies or felt discouraged. With his typical mule-like determination, he decided to lend a hoof.

Max became a tutor extraordinaire, offering his assistance to those who needed it. He patiently explained math problems, acted out history lessons, and even helped his classmates with their essays, providing creative and humorous ideas that left their teachers in stitches.

Under Max's guidance, the students gained confidence and began to excel in their studies. The school's academic achievements soared, and Max's impact became legendary.

But as the school year drew to a close, Max realized that he couldn't stay at the school forever. His true home was among the rolling hills, where he could frolic freely and explore to his heart's content.

With a heavy heart and a hint of nostalgia, Max bid farewell to his classmates and teachers. The entire school gathered to bid him a fond farewell, their laughter mixed with tears of gratitude.

As Max trotted down the road, his hooves leaving a cloud of dust behind him, he looked back at the school, a smile on his face. Max returned to the rolling hills, where he resumed his role as the town's beloved mule. The children would often visit, regaling him with tales of their own school adventures. Max would listen with a knowing grin, his heart filled with pride.

THE CAT WHO WAS STUCK UNDER THE MAT

Whiskers had an uncanny knack for getting into silly and hilarious situations. Little did he know that his latest adventure—a cat getting stuck under the mat—would lead to a laugh-out-loud tale that would have everyone in the cottage rolling with laughter.

Whiskers spotted a fluffy new welcome mat at the entrance of the cottage. Now, Whiskers had a mischievous curiosity that could not be contained, and he couldn't resist the urge to explore this new addition to his domain.

With a playful leap, Whiskers pounced onto the mat, but much to his surprise, it had a hidden secret. The mat had a mind of its own and, like a ravenous monster, it engulfed poor Whiskers, leaving only his twitching tail visible.

"Meow! Help!" cried Whiskers, his voice muffled under the mat.

The cottage inhabitants—a kind-hearted family named the Johnsons—rushed to the commotion. Mrs. Johnson, with her gentle nature, knelt down to investigate the peculiar sight before her. As she lifted the mat, Whiskers burst out, his fur standing on end, and ran off in a frantic dash.

The Johnsons couldn't help but laugh at the absurdity of the situation. They nicknamed the mat "The Mysterious Cat Trap" and resolved to keep an eye on Whiskers' misadventures.

But Whiskers, being the adventurous feline that he was, didn't let the incident deter him. He saw it as a challenge—a battle of wits between himself and the mat.

Every day, Whiskers would devise elaborate plans to outsmart the mat. He would practice his stealthy moves, studying the mat's every twist and turn, like a master detective on a mission.

One day, armed with a mouse-shaped toy and a twinkle in his eye, Whiskers launched his grand plan. With a nimble leap, he pounced onto the mat, cunningly distracting it with the toy as he tried to make his escape.

But much to his dismay, the mat wrapped itself around Whiskers tighter than ever, transforming him into a furry burrito.

"Meow!" Whiskers squeaked, his voice barely audible beneath the mat.

The Johnsons burst into laughter, their sides aching with amusement. They gently unravelled the mat, freeing Whiskers from his temporary confinement.

Undeterred by his failed attempt, Whiskers resolved to try again. He sought advice from the wiser creatures of the neighbourhood, like the wise old owl perched high on a tree and the wily fox who always had a trick up his sleeve.

Armed with their wisdom, Whiskers devised a new plan. He would use the element of surprise—a tactic that even the mat wouldn't expect.

With a burst of feline energy, Whiskers pounced onto the mat, this time armed with a feather tickler. He expertly tickled the mat's edges, confusing and disorienting it. While the mat convulsed with laughter (if mats could laugh, that is), Whiskers slipped out, victorious!

The Johnsons erupted into applause, their laughter filling the cottage. They marvelled at Whiskers' determination and quick thinking.

But as Whiskers basked in his triumph, he couldn't help but notice that the mat looked a little lonely, lying there without a cat to trap. So, with a mischievous twinkle in his eye, Whiskers devised a prank to include the mat in his mischief.

Late one evening, as the Johnsons gathered for a family movie night, Whiskers stealthily tiptoed into the living room, dragging the mat behind him. He carefully placed it on the floor, right behind Mr. Johnson's favourite armchair.

As Mr. Johnson settled into his seat, completely unaware of Whiskers' mischievous plot, he felt a sudden jolt. The mat had sprung to life, wrapping itself around his feet, trapping him like a fly in a spider's web.

The Johnsons burst into laughter, their voices echoing through the room. Whiskers, the master prankster, emerged from his hiding place, triumphantly patting himself on the back.

From that day forward, the mat and Whiskers formed an unlikely alliance. They entertained the Johnsons with their hilarious pranks and mischievous escapades, bringing laughter and joy to the cottage.

Made in United States
Orlando, FL
12 September 2023